Editors

Kim Fields

Heather Douglas

Illustrators

Kevin McArthy

Clint McKnight

Cover Artist

Brenda DiAntonis

Editor in Chief

Karen J. Goldfluss, M.S. Ed.

Art Production Manager

Kevin Barnes

Art Coordinator

Renée Christine Yates

Imaging

Nathan P. Rivera

Rosa C. See

Publisher

Mary D. Smith, M.S. Ed.

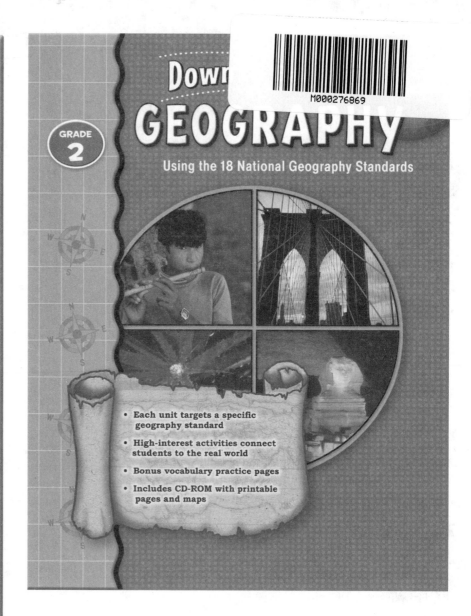

GRADE 2

Down... GEOGRAPHY

Using the 18 National Geography Standards

- Each unit targets a specific geography standard
- High-interest activities connect students to the real world
- Bonus vocabulary practice pages
- Includes CD-ROM with printable pages and maps

Author

Ruth Foster, M.Ed.

Teacher Created Resources, Inc.

6421 Industry Way

Westminster, CA 92683

www.teachercreated.com

ISBN: 978-1-4206-9272-1

© 2008 Teacher Created Resources, Inc.

Made in U.S.A.

Teacher Created Resources

Table of Contents

Introduction

Geography Today

It has been said that our world is becoming smaller, largely due to advanced communication, economic partnerships, and world trade markets. To understand, and eventually compete in, today's world, students must know more than physical characteristics of land and country borders. They must understand how communities and people interact, in part due to the geography of where they live. Students must understand that human actions can modify the physical environment and that changes occur in the use and importance of resources.

The goal of *Down to Earth Geography* is to help students become more geographically literate and better prepared for the global community. A variety of activities and high-interest readings take students on a journey that brings the world to them. At the end of the journey, students will have been introduced to the world of geography. In addition, they will have developed skills in assessing and understanding the world in spatial terms, places and regions, physical systems, human systems, environment and society, and the uses of geography.

About This Book

The units in this book are based on the National Geography Standards, which were developed by the Geography Education Standards Project and sponsored by the National Council of Geographic Education, the National Geography Society, the American Geographical Society, and the Association of American Geographers. These standards can be found in the book, Geography for Life: National Geography Standards, 1994.

Down to Earth Geography is divided into 18 units. Each unit focuses on one of the 18 National Geography Standards listed on pages 6–7.

How to Use This Book

Information Pages

Each unit begins with an introductory page that explains basic information about the unit. The information on this page is written on a level that allows students to read about the topics addressed in the unit. It provides them with both useful and interesting information to whet their appetites for future learning.

The Information Page also introduces the vocabulary words that are used in each unit. Vocabulary words are bolded when they are first introduced in an activity. It is recommended that vocabulary words be discussed and defined when they appear in an activity, rather than out of context. (A reproducible Geography Word Log is provided on page 166 to be used for recording the vocabulary words and meanings as they appear in context. Students can write the words and meanings on the log. Reproduce copies as needed.) Vocabulary Practice activities for each unit can be found on pages 156–164.

The What I Do section on the Information Page gives students brief directions for the unit activities and summarizes the new knowledge they will gain after completing the unit.

Activity Pages

The activities in each unit vary in form and are written to inspire students to think about and respond to the content. Some activities require students to mark areas on maps. Others require answering multiple choice, true/false, or fill-in questions. Several exercises ask students to write sentences or list reasons to support their choices.

Although the activities are written at a level that allows students to complete them independently, it is recommended that teachers use a combination of independent, small group, and whole-class learning approaches for each unit. Sharing information, ideas, and responses to the activities will reinforce the students' understanding of each standard.

An Answer Key for the Activity Pages is provided on pages 153–155.

How to Use This Book (cont.)

Reproducible Pages

Reproducible Pages are included at the end of this book (see pages 166–176). This section includes a world map, a map of each continent, two versions of a U.S. map, and two types of compasses. Copy and distribute these pages for student reference (e.g., for an Activity that includes locating a specific country or capital city in Africa, page 167 would be an excellent resource).

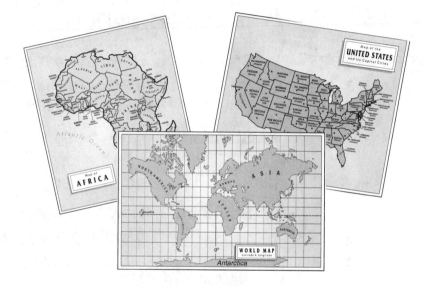

CD-ROM

Each CD-Rom includes all student pages and each reference map at the end of the book.

The student pages have been prepared as PDF files and can be printed from the CD. Print a master copy and reproduce as many as needed on a copier, or print as many copies as you wish right from the CD files. Pages are listed by the page numbers in the book and by the standards to which they are correlated. For example, **P_009 Standard 1** indicates that the content is from page 9, which appears in the standard 1 unit.

For printers capable of printing on transparency sheets, you can select specific student pages and maps to display on an overhead projector for whole-class viewing, discussion, or review.

The National Geography Standards

There are 18 National Geography Standards. All 18 standards are covered in this book. Each standard is covered in one unit. Each unit has a series of Activity exercises. The Activity exercises were designed to meet student expectations as listed by the National Geography Standards. Listed below and on page 7 are the standards taught and reinforced in this book.

The World in Spatial Terms

Standard 1: How to use maps and other geographic representations, tools, and technologies to acquire, process, and report information

Standard 2: How to use mental maps to organize information about people, places, and environments

Standard 3: How to analyze the spatial organization of people, places, and environments

Places and Regions

Standard 4: The physical and human characteristics of a place

Standard 5: That people create regions to interpret Earth's complexity

Standard 6: How culture and experience influence people's perception of places and regions

Physical Systems

Standard 7: The physical processes that shape the patterns of Earth's surface

Standard 8: The characteristics and spatial distribution of ecosystems on Earth's surface

The National Geography Standards *(cont.)*

Standards

9–18

Human Systems

Standard 9: The characteristics, distribution, and migration of human populations on Earth's surface

Standard 10: The characteristics, distributions, and complexity of Earth's cultural mosaics

Standard 11: The patterns and networks of economic interdependence on Earth's surface

Standard 12: The process, patterns, and functions of human settlement

Standard 13: How forces of cooperation and conflict among people influence the division and control of Earth's surface

Environment and Society

Standard 14: How human actions modify the physical environment

Standard 15: How physical systems affect human systems

Standard 16: The changes that occur in the meaning, use, distribution, and importance of resources

The Uses of Geography

Standard 17: How to apply geography to interpret the past

Standard 18: To apply geography to interpret the present and plan for the future

Maps, Globes, and Finding Our Way Around

What I Need to Know

Vocabulary

- eclipse
- globe
- map
- title
- key
- legend
- symbol
- compass
- scale

About Maps

Where do you live? Where is your school? Where is a big river? Whose desk is next to yours? Maps are tools that help us answer questions about where things are. They can show where people live. They can show where schools are located. They can show rivers. They can show who sits next to whom. They are good tools that can help us know where to go.

Our world is round, but maps are flat. We read maps. Maps have certain parts that help us read them. The parts help us know what the map is for and where things are. The parts help us know how far it is between different places.

What I Do

Read and complete each Activity. When you are done, you will know how to tell the Earth is round, how a globe and a map are different, and where the compass was invented.

Name _____   **Date** _____

Activity 1

People said, "Earth is flat. It is not round. The sky is a half circle. The half circle is above Earth. The sun moves. We see it move. It moves across the sky. The moon moves. We see it move. It moves across the sky. The stars move. We see them move. They move across the sky."

People were wrong. It is Earth that is moving. Earth is round like a circle.

How do we know?

Aristotle lived long ago. He saw an **eclipse**. This is when the moon passes into Earth's shadow. Earth's shadow on the moon was round! Only round things cast round shadows. Aristotle said, "Earth's shadow on the moon is round. Only a round thing can cast a round shadow. Earth is round."

Aristotle knew that Earth is round because

  A. we see it move

  B. it casts a round shadow

  C. the sky is a half circle

  D. Aristotle lived long ago

Draw shadows for the objects.

 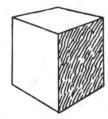  

Name _____ **Date** _____

Activity 2

A **globe** is round. A globe is a round model of Earth. Using a globe, we can see where the land and water are. A globe is a good tool.

A **map** is a tool, too. A map is flat. A map shows where land and water are. Globes show the true shape of land and water better than a flat map. This is because a globe is round like Earth.

Which is easier to fit into your pocket?

 A. a map   **B.** a globe

People use maps for many reasons. Which answer is not a reason people use maps?

 A. Maps are flat.   **C.** Maps show the land and water.

 B. Maps are easy to carry.   **D.** Maps are round like Earth.

Color the globe and map. Color the water blue. Color the land green. Put an **X** where you live.

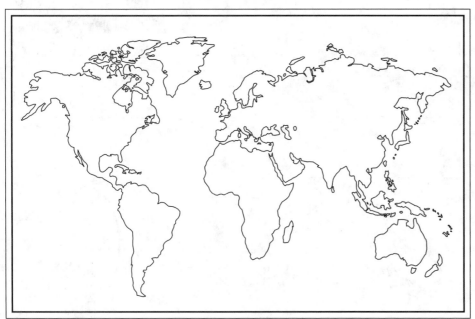

Name _____ **Date** _____

Activity 3

How do we know what a map is about? A map **title** is a name. The title tells us what the map is about.

How do we know what things are on a map? We use a **key**. A key is also known as a **legend**. We look at the map key or map legend. We see **symbols**. A symbol stands for something. The map key tells us what the symbols mean. The symbols tell us where the things are on the map.

Look at the map.

Circle the title. Underline the key or legend. Put a box around the symbol for tree.

Make a map of your classroom. Write a title for your map. Make a key or legend. Use three or more symbols in your key.

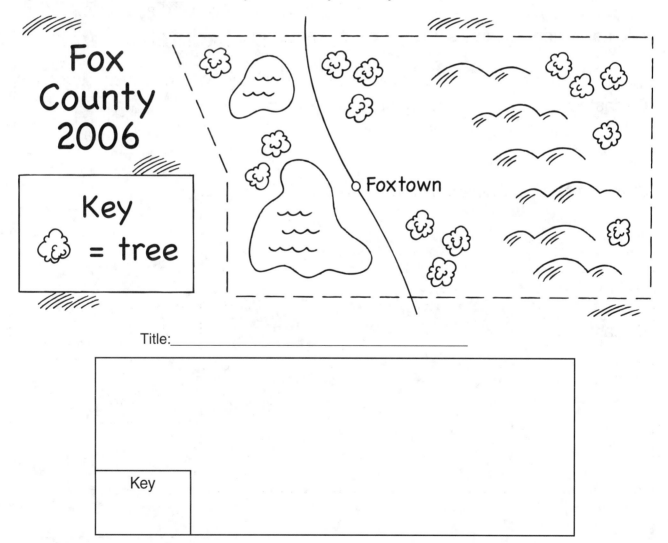

Title:_____

Name _____ **Date** _____

Activity 4

A **compass** is a tool. A compass shows directions. It shows north, south, east, and west. Often, we use *N* for north. We use *S* for south. We use *E* for east. We use *W* for west. We use a compass to know which way to go.

Where was the compass invented? The compass was invented in China long ago.

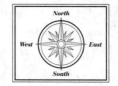 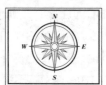

Write the directions on the two maps.

Which direction is the school from Henry's house?

A. north   **B.** south

C. east   **D.** west

Which direction is Henry's house from the school?

A. north   **B.** south

C. east   **D.** west

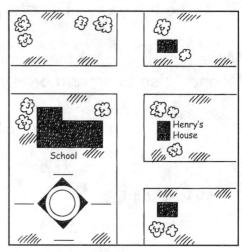

Which direction is China from where you live?

A. north

B. south

C. east

D. west

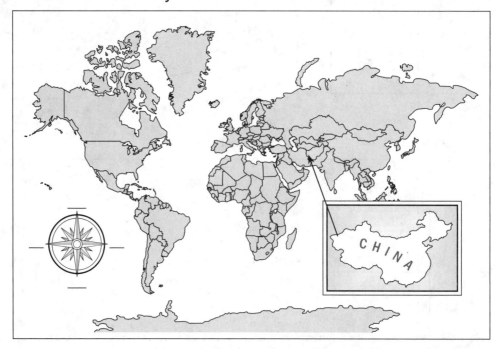

Name _____ **Date** _____

Activity 5

Start at the big dot. Do not pick up your pencil as you draw.

Go south two spaces.

Go west three spaces.

Go north two spaces.

Go east three spaces.

Which figure did you draw?

  A. square   **B.** circle   **C.** triangle   **D.** rectangle

Start at the white circle. Do not pick up your pencil as you draw.

Go east four spaces.

Go west two spaces.

Go south five spaces.

Go east two spaces.

Go west four spaces.

Which letter did you draw?

  A. T   **B.** H   **C.** I   **D.** C

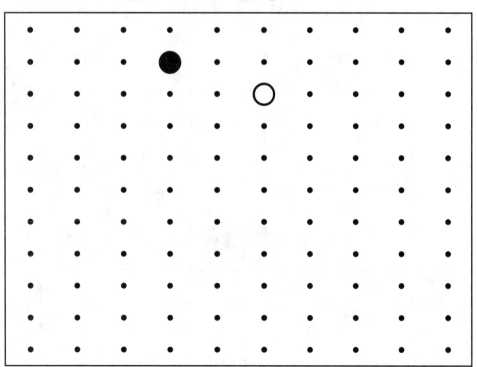

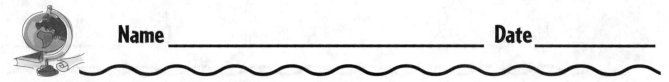

Name_____ **Date**_____

Activity 6

How far is the school from Jo's house? How far is the store from Jo's house? How far away is the fire station? How far away is the park?

Look at the map **scale.** The map scale shows us distance. An inch on the map means one mile in the real world. One inch on the map is a distance of one mile. Two inches on the map is two miles. Ten inches on the map is ten miles.

On the map, measure the number of inches from Jo's house to the school. Measure from Jo's house to the store. Measure from Jo's house to the fire station. Measure from Jo's house to the park. Write how far each place is from Jo's house.

	INCHES ON MAP	REAL DISTANCE IN MILES
school		
store		
fire station		
park		

Why are maps drawn to scale? Why aren't they drawn life-size?_____

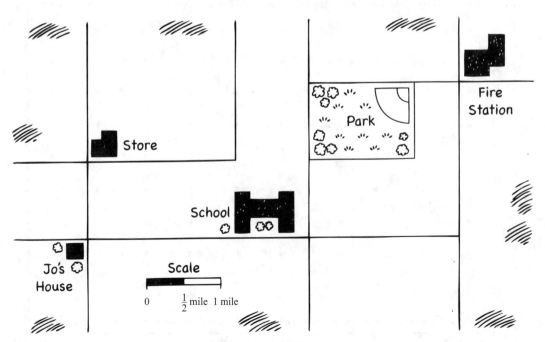

Name _____ **Date** _____

Activity 7

Look at the map. It is a map to school. It shows how Pete goes to school. Pete rides a bus.

Write how the bus takes Pete to school. Fill in the directions on the compass. Then write *north, south, east*, or *west* in the spaces below. Start from Pete's house.

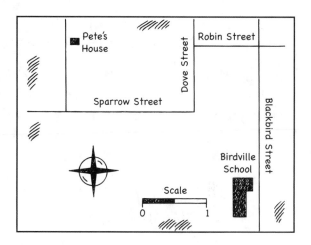

Go _____ to Sparrow Street.

Go _____ to Dove Street.

Go _____ to Robin Street.

Go _____ to Blackbird Street.

Go _____ to Birdville School.

About how many miles does Pete ride the bus to school? _____

Pete's school is east of the Mississippi River. Is your school east or west of the Mississippi River? _____

Mental Maps and Knowing Where We Are

What I Need to Know

Vocabulary

- mental map
- continent
- Africa
- Antarctica
- North America
- Asia
- Europe
- Australia
- South America

What I Do

About Mental Maps

We have lots of maps in our head. These maps are called mental maps. Our mental maps help us find our way. They help us find our way to school. They help us find our way to our neighbor's house.

The world is made up of continents. There are seven continents. We can make a map in our head of the world. We can think of where the continents are in our head. Our world map in our head helps us know where people live. It helps us know where animals live. It helps us know how the world fits together.

Read and complete each Activity. When you are done, you will know about an animal with two thumbs on each hand, a different animal that has eyes, ears, and nostrils on top of its head, and an animal that can knock a moose off its feet. You will also know what continents these animals live on.

Name _____ **Date** _____

Activity 1

You walked into the school. You went to your classroom. How did you know where to go? Did you look at a map? You did not look at a map. You did not need to because you used a map in your head. You used a **mental map**.

Draw a map. The map should be a school map. It should be like the map you used in your head. On the map, show the doors you used to walk into the school. Show the way to your classroom. Use a dotted line to show the way you walked.

If you can, draw other rooms and places in your school. You might draw:

- a cafeteria
- a library
- an office
- a playground
- restrooms
- classrooms

Put in all the places you can find with the map in your head.

Name _____   **Date** _____

Activity 2

A **continent** is a big land mass. There are seven continents in the world. Begin to make a mental map of the continents. To start, write the names of the continents where they should go.

Hippo ears, eyes, and nostrils are all on top of its head. Why? The hippo is very big. It can hide under the water. Only the top of its head shows. Hippos live in **Africa**. Draw some eyes, ears, and nostrils on the top of Africa.

You live on land. Your nostrils are open. Seals live mostly in the water. Seal nostrils are closed! Seals have a special muscle. The muscle opens their nostrils. Seals use the muscle when they want to breathe.

Many seals live in the cold waters around Antarctica. Draw a seal next to **Antarctica**.

How many continents are there?

  A. 5   **B.** 6   **C.** 7   **D.** 8

Which animal's nostrils are on top of its head?

  A. hippo   **B.** seal

Which animal has to use a special muscle to open its nostrils?

  A. hippo   **B.** seal

Name _____ **Date** _____

Activity 3

Wolverines live in **North America**. They use their noses to smell other animals. They are good trackers. Wolverines will climb trees and wait. They jump on big animals when they pass by. They can knock moose off their feet!

Wolverines are in the same family as skunks. Wolves and bears leave wolverines alone. Why? Wolverines stink! They are also strong fighters.

Work on your mental map of the continents. Look at the map below. Think about where Africa goes. Think about where Antarctica goes. Think about where North America goes. Write the three continent names where you think they should go. Check your answers. You may change them if you need to.

Wolverines are in the same family as

  A. bears   **B.** wolves   **C.** skunks   **D.** moose

Write *north, south, east*, or *west* in the spaces below.

Antarctica is _____of North America.

North America is _____ of Africa.

Africa is _____ of Antarctica.

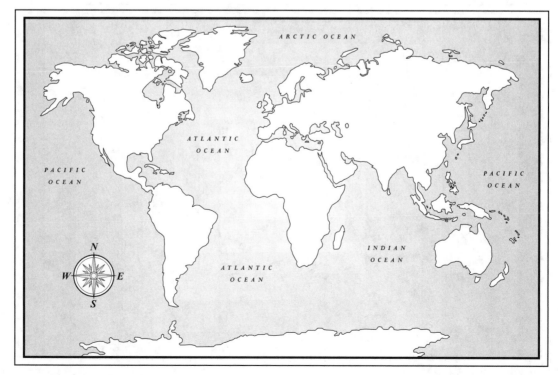

Name _____ **Date** _____

Activity 4

Tigers used to live all across *Asia*. Now they only live in small parts. Tigers live alone. Sometimes tigers will share their food. How do they let other tigers know they have food to share? They roar. The roar can be heard over a mile (2 km) away!

Tigers do not live in *Europe*, but Asia and Europe share a border. Mountains separate them. The Ural Mountains separate them.

Work on your mental map of the continents. On the map, write the names of the continents of Africa, Antarctica, North America, Asia, and Europe. Check your answers. Change them if you need to.

The Ural Mountains are between

A. Asia and Africa   **C.** Asia and Antarctica

B. Asia and Europe   **D.** Asia and North America

Write *north*, *south, east*, or *west*.

Europe is _____ of Africa.

Europe is _____ of Asia.

Europe is _____ of North America.

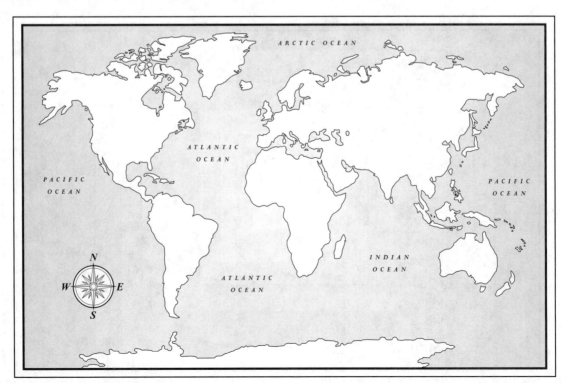

Name _____ **Date** _____

Activity 5

Koala bears live in **Australia**. Koalas live in eucalyptus trees. Koalas eat leaves. They only eat eucalyptus leaves. They do not drink much water. They get most of their water from the tree leaves. Koalas rarely fall out of the trees. How do they hold on so well? Koalas have two thumbs on each hand!

The anaconda snake does not have two thumbs. It does not even have hands! But sometimes the anaconda snake climbs trees. It eats birds. It eats other animals in the trees. It also lies in the water. It catches animals that come to drink. One anaconda weighed 600 pounds (272 kg)! Anacondas live in
South America.

Work on your mental map of the continents. On the map, write the name of each continent. Check your answers. Change them if you need to.

How many thumbs do you have on each hand? _____

Do you weigh more or less than the anaconda in the story? _____

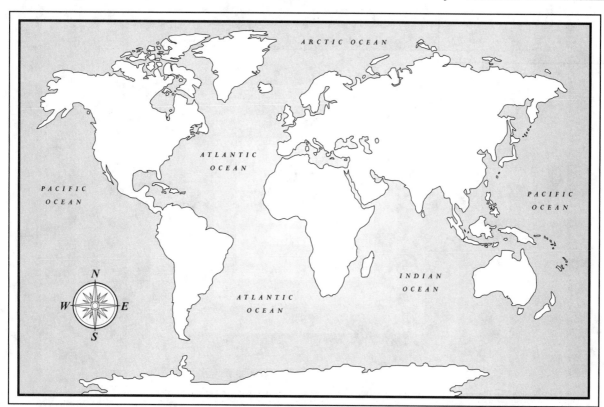

Name _____ **Date** _____

Activity 6

Be a mapmaker. Do not look at other maps! You may look at other maps later.

Make an outline of all the continents. Write the continent names.

Now you may check your map. Make changes if you need to.

1. Make a title for your map.

2. Make a key for your map. Your key should have two symbols. The symbols may be colors. One symbol will show land. One symbol will show water.

3. Put a compass on your map.

Write the name of the missing continent.

_____ is north of South America and west of Europe.

_____ is east of South America and south of Europe.

Title: _____

Key

Name _____ **Date** _____

Activity 7

What country do you live in? _____

Do you live in the United States? _____

Do you live in Canada? _____   Do you live in Mexico? _____

In your head, you should have a map. The map should be a picture of your country. Find your country on the map. Trace its outline.

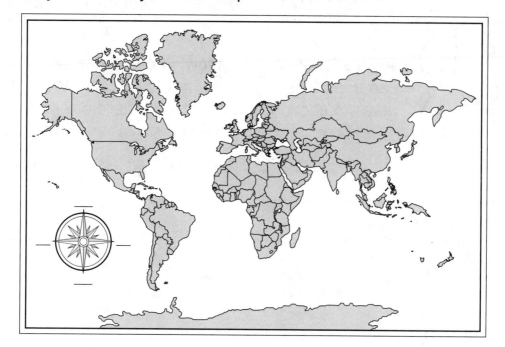

Close your eyes. Picture your country's outline. Now, open your eyes. Draw the outline of your country. It does not need to be perfect.

Write the name of your country in your outline.

Around your outline, write the countries that border (or touch) your country.

Directions and Where Things Are

What I Need to Know

Vocabulary

- density

About Where Things Are

Think about where you live. You live on a street. People live all around you. Some live to the north. Some live to the south. Some live to the west. Some live to the east. We can tell where people live by looking at certain kinds of maps.

We can use maps to show where things come from. We can use maps to show where cities are. We can use maps to show how many things there are in one area.

What I Do

Read and complete each Activity. When you are done, you will have seen different kinds of maps. You will have seen a street map, a subway map, and a zoo map. You will be able to tell where things are on maps.

Name _____   **Date** _____

Activity 1

Dan lives in Fruitville. Look at the map of Fruitville. Find Dan's house.

Dan's house is on

A. Apple Street   **C.** Cherry Street

B. Orange Street   **D.** Banana Street

Which place is on Dan's street?

A. school   **C.** post office

B. hospital   **D.** fire station

Write *north, south, east,* or *west*.

The school is _____ of Dan's house.

The hospital is _____ of the school.

Hospital

School

Banana

Apple   Street

Fruitville   Cherry

Dan's
House

Fire
Station

N
W   E
S

Orange   Street

Street   Street

Post
Office

Name _____ **Date** _____

Activity 2

Look at the map. Find Antberg. Find Beeberg. Find Butterflyberg.

Which place would be the easiest to visit?

A. Antberg

B. Beeberg

C. Butterflyberg

Why? _____

Which place would be the hardest to visit?

A. Antberg

B. Beeberg

C. Butterflyberg

Why? _____

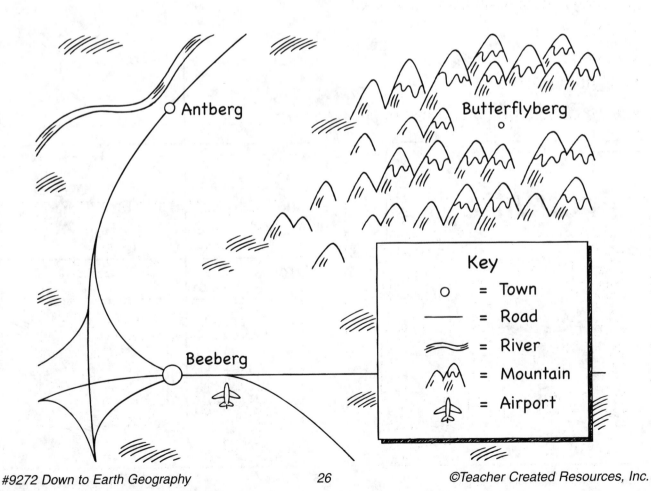

Name _____   **Date** _____

Activity 3

Use the map from Activity 2 on page 26. Not many people go to Butterflyberg.

What might make it so more people go to Butterflyberg?

A. an airport built in Antberg

B. a bigger airport built in Beeberg

C. a big road built from Antberg to Beeberg

D. a bridge and road built from Antberg to Butterflyberg

One city has five schools. One city has two schools. One city has one school.

Which city probably has the most schools?

A. Antberg

B. Beeberg

C. Butterflyberg

One city has 50 stores. One city has 10 stores. One city has 2 stores.

Which city most likely has 10 stores?

A. Antberg

B. Beeberg

C. Butterflyberg

How do people get in and out of your area? _____

_____

Name _____ **Date** _____

Activity 4

Look at the subway map. Henry is getting on at Oak Station. He wants to go to Main Street Station.

Which train should Henry get on?

A. Train A

B. Train B

C. Train C

D. Train D

Henry is meeting his friend. He is meeting his friend at Main Street Station. Then the two children are going to the Children's Museum.

How many stops away is the museum from Main Street Station?

A. 1   **C.** 3

B. 2   **D.** 4

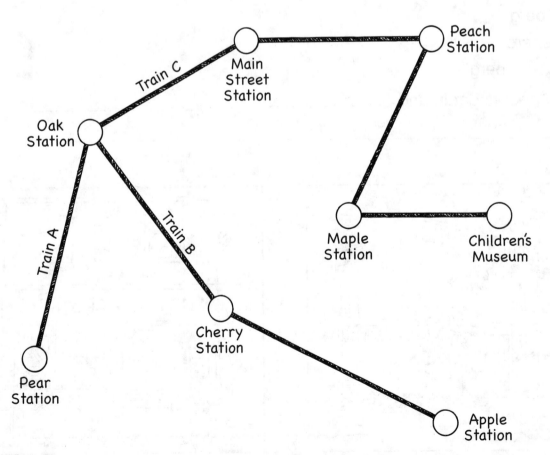

Name _____ **Date** _____

Activity 5

Tamay did a house count. She wanted to know the number of houses in her area. She wanted to know where the most houses were, too. She wanted to know the density of the houses. Density is how many persons or things are in an area.

To show density, Tamay made a map. She put a grid on the map. Color the squares for Tamay.

Color the squares with:

- 0 to 3 houses red
- 4 to 5 houses blue

- 7 to 9 houses green
- 10 to 12 houses yellow

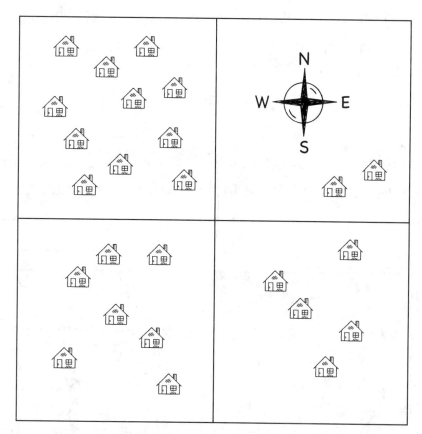

From the map, you can tell that the density of houses is greatest in the _____ .

A. east

C. west

Why might a city planner want to keep track of house density? _____

Name _____ **Date** _____

Activity 6

Friday was fruit day.

Pang brought blueberries. The blueberries were grown in Maine.

Vina brought apples. The apples were grown in Washington State.

Lita brought cherries. The cherries were grown in Oregon.

Akio brought grapes. The grapes were grown in California.

Kaya brought oranges. The oranges were grown in Florida.

Alberto brought pineapples. The pineapples were grown in Hawaii.

Brian brought peaches. The peaches were grown in Georgia.

Look at the map. Find and label your state. Find and label the states the fruit came from.

How do you think the fruit got to your state?

_____

How long do you think it took to get to your state? _____

Do you think people could buy these fruits in your state long ago? Why or why not?_____

_____

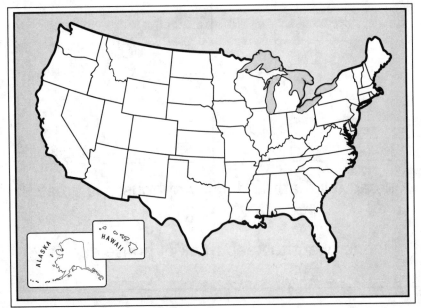

Name _____ **Date** _____

Activity 7

Look at the map. It is a zoo map.

The restroom and food area is:

in front of the _____

next to the _____

The koalas are:

behind the _____

next to the _____

The seals are:

in front of the _____

behind the _____

next to the _____

The birds are:

between the _____ and _____

_____

in front of _____

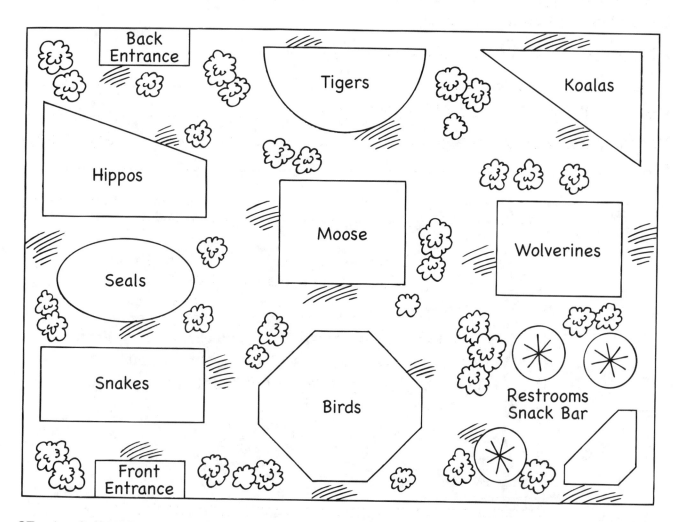

Different Places, Different People

About Different Places and People

Some places are hot. Some places are cold. The places have different regions, or areas. Different plants and animals live in different regions.

Regions shape what people do and how they live. Some regions are good places to grow food. In some regions, it is too cold or too hot to grow food. More people live in some regions than in other regions.

What I Need to Know

Vocabulary

- erode
- desert
- nomad
- region
- polar
- prairie
- plain
- cool grasslands
- tropical grasslands
- valley

What I Do

Read and complete each Activity. When you are done, you will know how an island was born, about different kinds of grasslands, and how you and a giraffe are alike.

Name _____ **Date** _____

Activity 1

In 1963, a cook was on a fishing boat. The cook saw smoke high in air. It was rising from the sea. The cook said, "A ship is on fire." A ship was not on fire. Where was the smoke coming from?

There was a volcano! The volcano was erupting. Lava was coming out. A new island was born. The island is called Surtsey. Surtsey is close to Iceland.

People looked at the island. They wanted to learn how living things get to new places. The first living thing landed when the island was six months old. It was a tiny insect. Then, some weevils came. Weevils are tiny beetles. The weevils came on wood. The wood floated to the island. The first plant was moss. Next, birds came.

On the map, find and label Iceland and Surtsey.

Surtsey is in which ocean?

A. Arctic Ocean

B. Indian Ocean

C. Pacific Ocean

D. Atlantic Ocean

How did the weevils get to the island?

A. They erupted in lava.

B. They came on birds.

C. They floated on wood.

D. They came on a fishing boat.

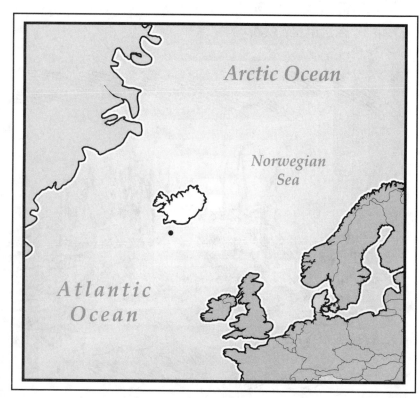

Name _____ **Date** _____

Activity 2

First, Surtsey was a round island. Then it changed after 1965. It changed to a pear-shaped island. (The number 8 looks a little like a pear.)

Draw a round circle. Draw a pear-shaped figure.

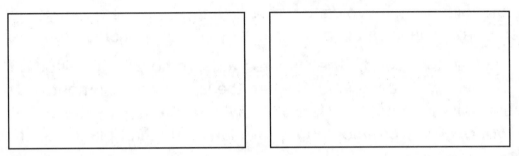

Why did Surtsey change? Winter storms came. The storms caused some parts of the island to **erode**. When something erodes, it is washed away. It is washed away by wind. It is washed away by water. Parts of the island were washed away. The parts were washed to other places on the island.

From the story, you can tell that when something erodes,

   A. it gets bigger

   B. it is an island

   C. it can change shape

   D. it is a winter storm

Name _____ **Date** _____

Activity 3

Think of a place. The place is hot. There are no rivers. There are no lakes.
There is little water. There is little rain. It is very dry. There is lots of sand.

What type of place is this?

A. a desert   **C.** a grassland

B. a forest   **D.** a rain forest

Look at the map. The map shows **deserts**. There are

deserts all around the world. Often, people who live

in deserts are **nomads**. Nomads do not stay in one place.

 They move from place to place.

Why might desert nomads move from place to place? They move

A. to find water   **C.** to find the hottest place

B. to see more sand   **D.** to see how far they can go

What type of house would be good for a nomad?

A. a wood house   **B.** a tent house   **C.** a stone house

Why would this be a good house for a nomad? _____

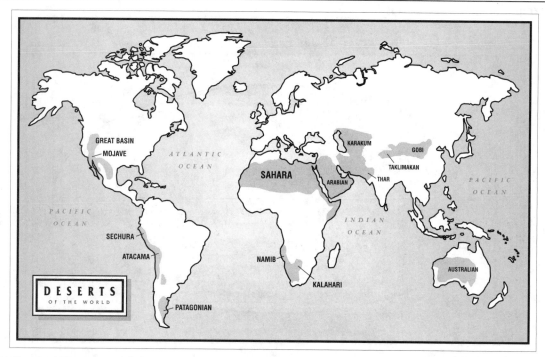

Name _____ **Date** _____

Activity 4

A **region** is a large area of land. **Polar** Regions are by the Poles. One Polar Region is by the North Pole. Another Polar Region is by the South Pole. There is lots of ice in Polar Regions. Everything is frozen.

It is a desert but it is not a hot desert. It is a frozen desert. All the water is frozen. It is too cold for clouds to form. Little snow or water falls from the sky.

How many people do you think live in the Polar Regions?

  A. a lot   **B.** very few

Give two reasons why:

   1. _____

   2. _____

Today, many people who work in Polar Regions bring food with them. The food comes by plane,
or by boat.

Why do you think they bring their own food?

  A. They do not have time to plant it.   B.   Plants cannot grow where everything is frozen.

On the map, find and label the North Pole and the South Pole.

Which Pole is closer to you? _____

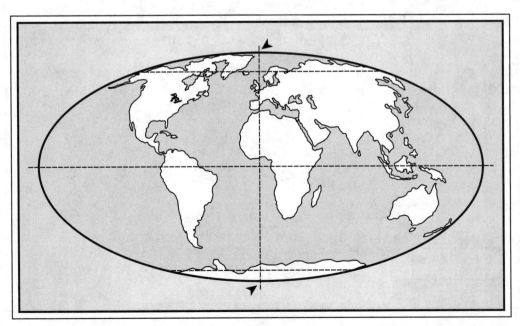

Name _____ **Date** _____

Activity 5

The Great Plains is a region in the United States. The Great Plains is a **prairie**. A prairie is a treeless **plain**. A plain is a nearly flat region of land. A prairie is made of grassland. The Great Plains is a **cool grassland** region. Cool grassland regions have warm summers and cold winters. Most cool grasslands have been changed. Why?

wheat   corn

Cool grasslands are good places to grow crops. Wheat and oats are grown. Corn and soybeans are grown. Wild animals used to eat the grass. Today, cows, sheep, horses, and goats eat the grass. They eat crops grown on the grasslands, too.

oats   soybeans

Which wild animal used to feed on the Great Plains?

A. cow   **B.** goat   **C.** sheep   **D.** buffalo

Bread is made from wheat. Where was the wheat grown?

A. hot desert   **B.** frozen desert   **C.** high mountains   **D.** cool grasslands

Color the Great Plains on the map.

Do you live on the Great Plains? _____

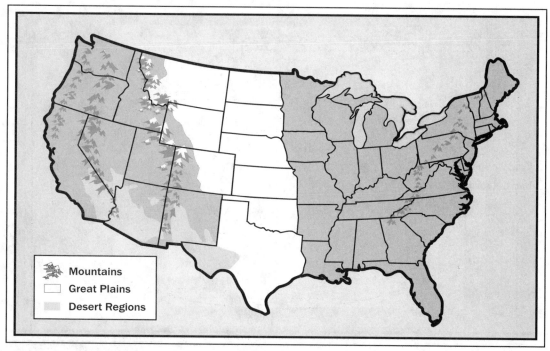

Mountains
Great Plains
Desert Regions

Name _____ **Date** _____

Activity 6

Some grasslands are not cool grasslands. They are **tropical grasslands**. Tropical places are warm. Tropical grasslands have tall grasses. It is warm all year. There is a wet season and a dry season. There are some trees. Zebras, lions, and giraffes live in tropical grasslands in Africa.

Zebras, lions, and giraffes live in a grassland region

  A. where it gets cool in the winter

  B. where there is a wet and dry season

You have seven bones in your neck. So does a giraffe! Most likely this means that

  A. a giraffe has the same sized neck as you

  B. a giraffe's neck bones are bigger than yours

On the map, use one color to shade in the cool grasslands. Use a different color to shade in the tropical grasslands.

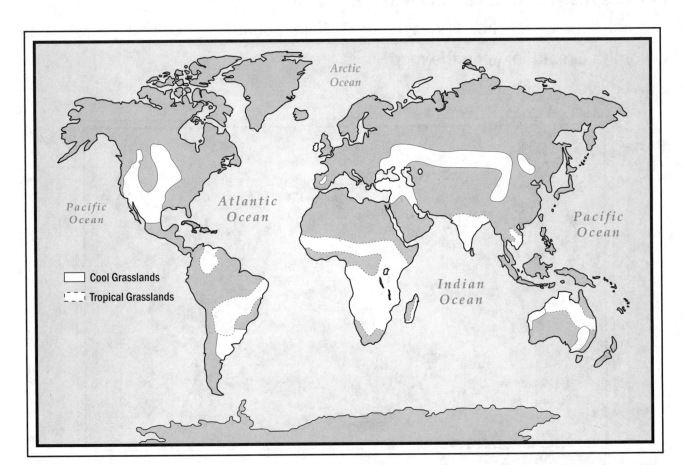

Name _____ **Date** _____

Activity 7

Look at the map. Look where people live.

Which thing do many people live by? (Pick two.)

   A. water   **B.** roads   **C.** deserts   **D.** mountains

What came first?

   A. living by roads   **B.** living by water

Why? _____

Long ago, people often settled in river valleys. A **valley** is a low place. A valley is often between hills or mountains.

People lived in a river valley because

   A. it was by water   **C.** it was between hills

   B. it was a low place   **D.** it was between mountains

What is the closest road to you? _____

Where does your water come from? _____

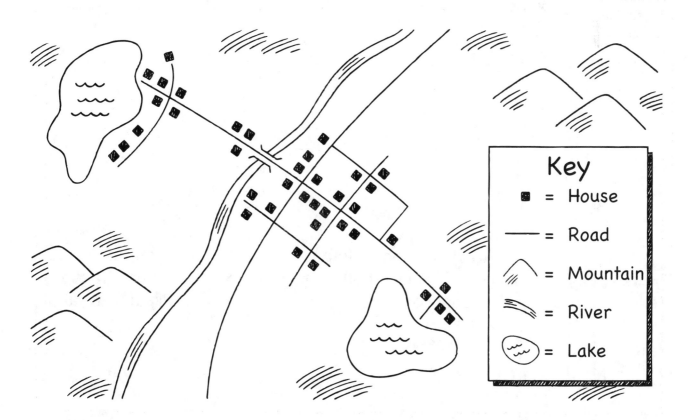

Places with Things in Common

What I Need to Know

Vocabulary

- goods
- canal
- coast
- ocean
- equator
- rain forest
- sea

About Places with Things in Common

The world is a big place. The world is made up of regions in different places. They are all around the world. Some regions are hot and some are cold. Some have special kinds of plants.

Over time, regions can change. People may change the places they live or settle by. They may build cities. They may build roads.

What I Do

Read and complete each Activity. When you are done, you will know about water streets, which country has the longest coastline in the world, and you will know what a sea is.

Name _____ **Date** _____

Activity 1

Venice is a city in Italy. On the map, find and label Italy and Venice.

What does Italy look like?

A. a hat   **B.** a coat

C. a boot   **D.** a shirt

There are no cars in Venice. There are no trucks.
Goods are things you can make or sell. How
are goods moved? How do people get around?
Venice is filled with **canals**. A canal is a ditch filled with water. People get
around on boats. They move goods by boat.

List some goods made or sold in your area or state.

_____

List some ways goods are moved and people get around in your area. _____

_____

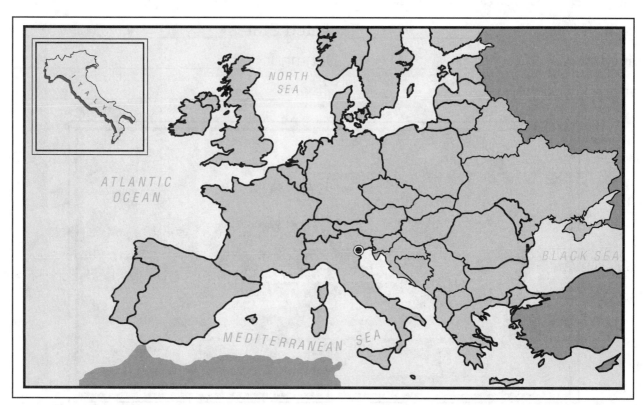

Name _____ **Date** _____

Activity 2

Think about a car. Think about driving. In most countries, on which side of the road do cars drive?

  A. left   **B.** right

In some places, you drive on the left. In other places you drive on the right.

On the map, find and color England, Pakistan, and Japan. These countries drive on the left.

On the map, find and color the United States, Denmark, and Mexico. These countries drive on the right.

Draw a picture. In your picture, have a road with a car on it. Which side will your car be on?

Using the map below, write which continent each country is part of.

England _____   United States _____

Pakistan _____   Denmark _____

Japan _____   Mexico_____

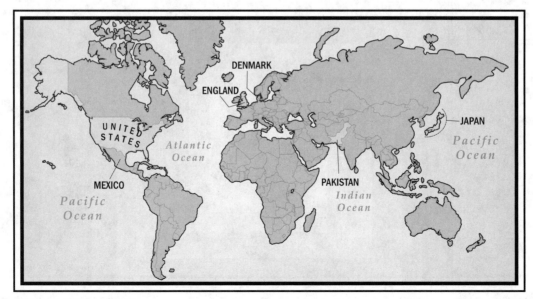

Name _____ **Date** _____

Activity 3

A **coast** is land along a body of water. Land along a coast is a coastal region.

Take all the people in the world. Put them in three groups. The groups are the same size. How many groups do you think live in coastal regions? Two of the groups live in coastal regions. On the bar, color two of the squares to show about how many people live in coastal regions.

Canada has the longest coastline of any country in the world. Find Canada on the map.

Which oceans does Canada border?_____

Alaska has the longest coastline of any state in the United States. Find Alaska on the map.

Which oceans does Alaska border?_____

Do you live in a coastal region? _____

What is the nearest coast to you? _____

Name _____ **Date** _____

Activity 4

An **ocean** is a large body of water. Oceans are salty. There are four oceans on Earth.

Color three parts of the circle blue. Color one part of the circle brown. The blue part shows how much of Earth is covered by water. The brown part shows how much of Earth is covered by land.

PACIFIC	ATLANTIC	INDIAN	ARCTIC
biggest	2nd biggest	warmest	smallest
deepest	most ship travel	coldest	

Which ocean is the smallest? _____

Which ocean is the warmest? _____

Which ocean is the biggest? _____

Which ocean has the most ship travel? _____

- On the map, write the name of each ocean.
- The Arctic Ocean is near the North Pole. (Write **ARC** on map.)
- The Indian Ocean is between Africa and Australia. (Write **I** on map.)
- The Pacific Ocean is between Asia and North America. (Write **P** on map.)
- The Atlantic Ocean is between Africa and North America. (Write **ATL** on map.)

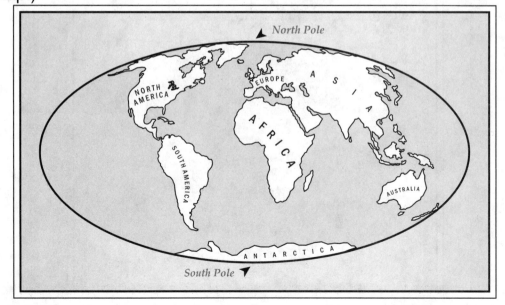

Name _____ **Date** _____

Activity 5

Tropical regions are found around the **equator**. What is the equator? The equator is a line. It is not real. It goes around the middle of Earth and divides it in two.

One country is named for the equator. The country is Ecuador. Ecuador is on the equator!

A large bird lives in Ecuador. It is the largest flying bird in the Americas. It is the Andean condor. How big is it? It can easily be 10 feet (3 m) from wingtip to wingtip. The condor eats dead
animals and dead fish. It lives high in the mountains.

Find Ecuador on the map.

Which continent is Ecuador on? _____

Which ocean does it border? _____

Do you live north or south of the equator? ___

Which two continents are completely south of the equator? _____

_____

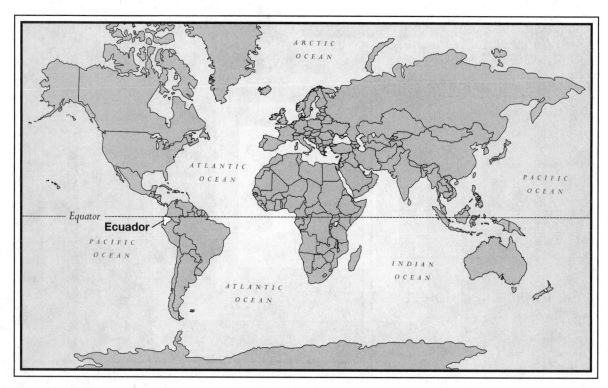

Name_____ **Date**_____

Activity 6

Tropical forests are found near the equator. Tropical forests are warm and wet. They are often called **rain forests**.

Honduras is a country with tropical rain forests. Some plants in Honduras do not live on the ground. They live on other plants. The plant makes a "cup" with its leaves. When it rains, the cup fills up! When the plants get big, the cups can hold 3 gallons (11 L) of water! High in the tree, insects will live in the water. Little animals will swim in and drink the water.

A **sea** is smaller than an ocean. A sea is connected to an ocean. A sea is salty. Honduras borders an ocean. It borders a sea too.

Find Honduras on the map.

Which sea does Honduras border?_____

Which ocean does Honduras border?_____

Is Honduras north or south of the equator? _____

Why isn't the water in the plant considered a sea? _____

_____

_____

_____

Color the tropical rain-forest regions.

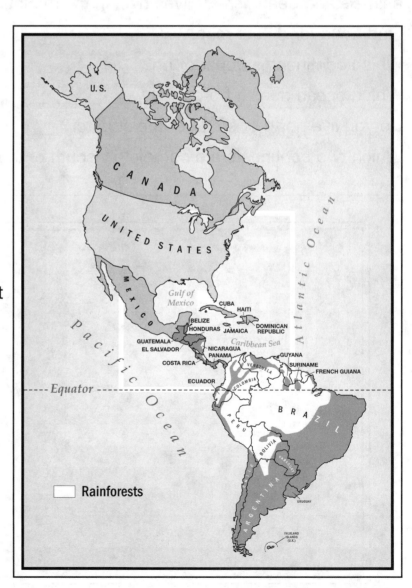

Name _____ **Date** _____

Activity 7

Tennessee is a state. A car factory was built in Tennessee. The factory needed a lot of workers. Some new people moved in to work in the factory. The people needed houses, stores, and their children needed schools. The region changed.

Think about where you live. Is there anything new? Are there new buildings? Are there new stores? New schools? New houses? New roads?

List three new things.

1. _____

2. _____

3. _____

List two jobs people do in your region that they did not do long ago.

1. _____

2. _____

Find Tennessee on the map.

Tennessee is _____ of North Carolina.

  A. north   **B.** south   **C.** east   **D.** west

North Carolina is _____Tennessee.

  A. north   **B.** south   **C.** east   **D.** west

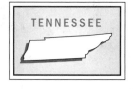

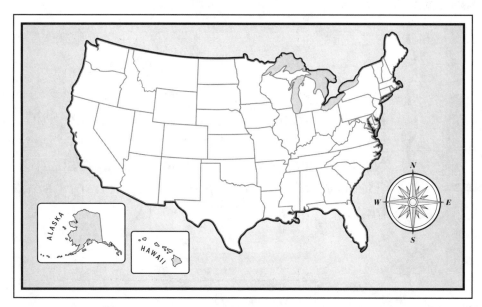

How We Think About Different Places and Where We Live

What I Need to Know

Vocabulary

- current
- gulf
- bay

What I Do

About How We Think About Different Places

The world is made up of different regions. The United States is made up of different regions, too. All people do not feel the same about places. We do not all like the same things. What is important to us may not be important to someone else. We need to know that not all people feel the same.

Read and complete each Activity. When you are done, you will know about an animal that is the fastest animal in North America. You will know about a state known as the "Beehive State," and if a gulf is bigger or smaller than a bay.

Name _____ **Date** _____

Activity 1

Think of four places. The places should be important. They do not need to be important to other people. They need to be important to you.

Make a map. Put your places on the map. Make these places the biggest. You can put anything else you want on the map, too.

Title: _____

Look at your classmates maps. Did you think the same things were important?

_____

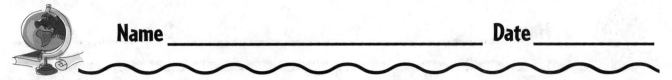

Name _____ **Date** _____

Activity 2

Think of a grown-up. It could be your mother. It could be your father. It could be your aunt. It could be your uncle. It could be any grown-up.

Now, think like a grown-up! Think of four places important to a grown-up. The places do not need to be important to you. They need to be important to a grown-up.

Make a map. Put the important places on the map. Make these places the biggest. You can put anything else you want on the map, too.

Title: _____

```


```

Look at the map. Look at the map from Activity 1. Are the important places the same? _____

Name _____　**Date** _____

Activity 3

Woody Guthrie was born in Oklahoma. He wrote over 1,000 songs. He wrote a song called
"This Land is Your Land." Read the words to the song.

This land is your land.
This land is my land.
From California to the New York Island,
From the Redwood Forest to the gulf stream waters,
This land was made for you and me. (©1945)

From the song, you can tell that Woody Guthrie

  A. feels people should buy and sell land

  B. feels that people should know about forests

  C. feels that the United States is a land for everyone

  D. feels that only California and New York are important

Redwood trees grow in the west.
They grow in

  A. New York　**B.** California

What kinds of trees grow in your state? _____

On the map, find and label Oklahoma (OK), California (CA), and New York (NY).

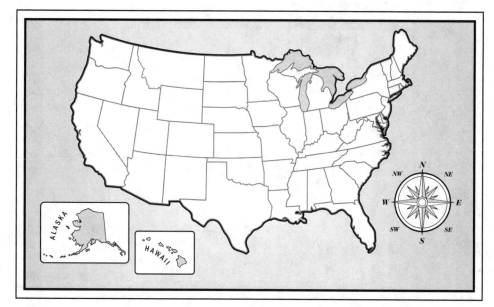

Name _____   **Date** _____

Activity 4

What is the Gulf Stream? The Gulf Stream is a **current**. A current is a "river."
It is a river of seawater that flows in the ocean. Some currents are warm water.
Some currents are cold water.

The Gulf Stream is a warm current. It flows at about 4 miles (6 km) per hour. It
starts in the Gulf of Mexico. It flows up to New York. A **gulf** is a large area of
sea that is partly surrounded by land. A gulf is bigger than a **bay**.

Which is not true about the Gulf Stream?

   A. It is a cold current.   **C.** It is a river of seawater.

   B. It flows in the ocean.   **D.** It starts in the Gulf of Mexico.

The ocean the Gulf Stream current flows into is the

   A. Arctic Ocean   **B.** Indian Ocean   **C.** Pacific Ocean   **D.** Atlantic Ocean

Find the Gulf of Mexico. Draw a line from the Gulf of Mexico to New York.

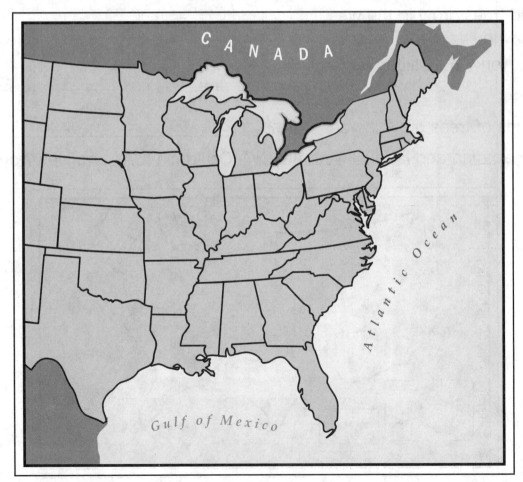

Name _____ **Date** _____

Activity 5

Your school needs many things. It is raising money. What should the school spend the money on? Take a vote! Everyone in your class can vote. Each person can vote for only two things. Make a bar graph to show the number of votes.

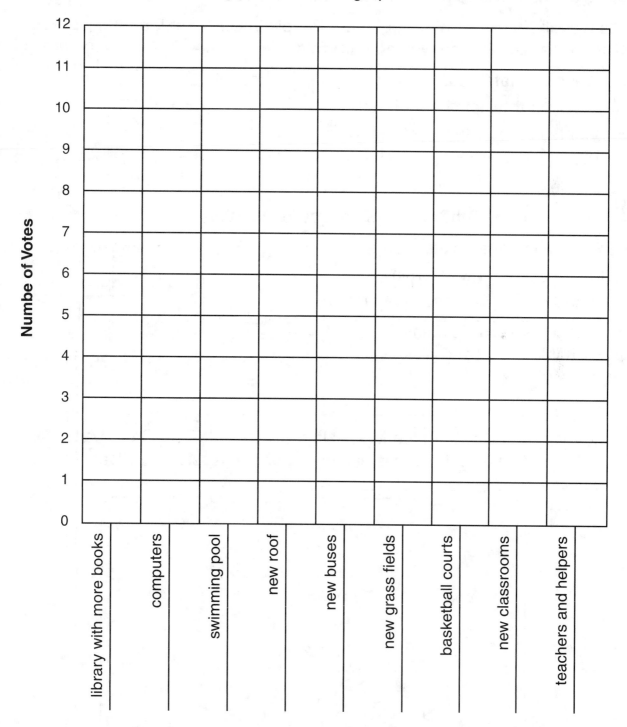

Do people think the same things are important? _____

Name _____ **Date** _____

Activity 6

The United States has 50 states. Each state has a nickname. Sometimes a nickname can help you know about a state.

Utah is a state. Utah's nickname is "Beehive State."

Bees work hard. Bees work together. People in Utah wanted to honor all the people who worked hard to settle their state.

The "Beehive State" is a good name for Utah because

A. people in the state honor bees

B. people in the state worked hard together

C. people in the state kept beehives

D. people in the state like nicknames

Utah is in a region of the United States called the West.

Which state is not a Western state?

A. Idaho   **C.** California

B. Oregon   **D.** West Virginia

What is your state's nickname?
Do you think it is a good nickname?
Why or why not? _____

On the map, find Utah and the Mississippi River. Color the Great Salt Lake. The Great Salt Lake is the largest lake west of the Mississippi River.

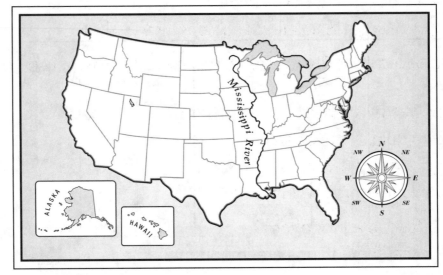

Name _____ **Date** _____

Activity 7

Read the letter.

> Dear Kit,
>
> I am in Kansas. Kansas is a state in the Midwest. I saw an animal. It was fast. It is the fastest animal in North America. It is a pronghorn. What is a pronghorn? It is like an antelope.
>
> They grow a lot of wheat here. They grow more than any other state. I like the "Breadbasket of America!"
>
> See you soon,
>
> Jay

How does Jay feel about Kansas?

   A. He likes the state.

   B. He wants to move to Kansas.

   C. He wishes it had more quick animals.

   D. He is going to stay in Kansas a long, long time.

Why is Kansas called the "Breadbasket of America"? Bread is made out of wheat, and

   A. pronghorns live in Kansas

   B. wheat grows quickly in Kansas

   C. Kansas is in North America

   D. Kansas grows the most wheat

Can you run as fast as a pronghorn? _____ (A pronghorn can run 60 miles [97 km] per hour.)

Patterns on Earth's Surface

About Earth's Patterns

Every day has 24 hours. But some days have more daylight hours than other days. Daylight hours take place because of how Earth moves. Earth spins around on its axis. It goes around the sun, too. The way Earth moves makes patterns. Knowing about the patterns helps us know what we can grow. It helps us know how things can change.

What I Need to Know

Vocabulary

- Arctic Circle
- Antarctic Circle
- axis
- tilts
- swamp
- canyon
- silt

What I Do

Read and complete each Activity. When you are done, you will know about places that are dark for many months and light for many other months. You will also learn about maps that show cold temperature areas.

Name _____ **Date** _____

Activity 1

Doug looked on a package of seeds. On the package was a map that showed zones. The seeds would not grow in every zone. They would only grow in some zones. Why?

The zones showed temperatures. They showed average cold temperatures. They did not show where it was hot. They only showed the average cold temperature.

Look at the maps. They are zone maps. One map is of California. One map is of North Dakota.

Which state has more average cold-temperature zones?

   A. California

   B. North Dakota

One state grows more than half the nation's fruits. It grows more than half the nuts. It grows more than half the vegetables. Think about the zone maps before you answer.

Which state grows more than half the nation's fruits and vegetables?

   A. California

   B. North Dakota

What is the average cold temperature for where you live? _____

What crops are grown in your state? _____

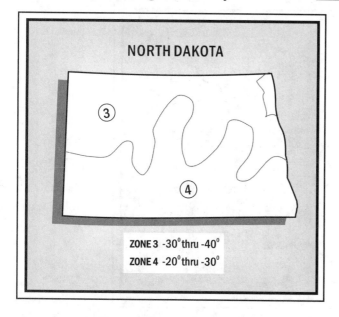

Name _____ **Date** _____

Activity 2

Doug lives in Minnesota. The seeds he wants to buy will grow in Zones 6, 7, and 8.

Will Doug's seeds grow in Minnesota?

  A. no

  B. yes

Look at the zone map for Mississippi. Will Doug's seeds grow in Mississippi?

  A. no

  B. yes

Which zone map looks most like North Dakota's zone map?

  A. Minnesota

  B. Mississippi

On the map, find Minnesota and Mississippi.

What would you guess looks most like Alabama's zone map? (Hint: Find where Alabama is on the map before you answer.)

  A. Minnesota

  B. Mississippi

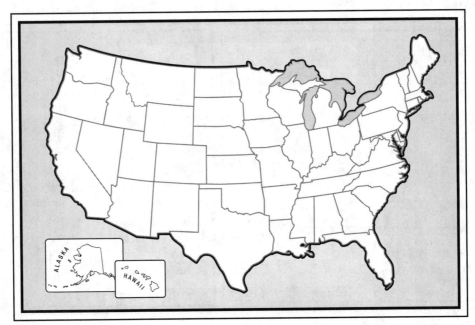

Name _____ **Date** _____

Activity 3

On the map, find the equator. Find the **Arctic Circle**.

Trace the Arctic Circle.

Circle one:

The Arctic Circle is by the (**North/South**) Pole.

Think about your day. You have light. You see the sun every day. In the summer, the days are long. You see the sun more hours. In the winter, the days are short. You see the sun fewer hours.

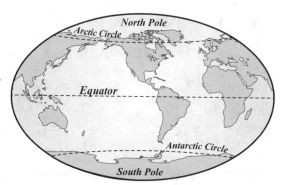

It is different above the Arctic Circle. How? The sun starts shining March 21st. It shines until September 21st. It never sets. It is light all day. It is light for six months.

What is it like the other days? It is dark. From September 22nd to March 20th, the sun never rises. It is dark for six months.

Look at the calendar. Color all the days it is light above the Arctic Circle.

January	February	March	April	May	June
S M T W TH F SA	S M T W TH F SA	S M T W TH F SA	S M T W TH F SA	S M T W TH F SA	S M T W TH F SA
1 2 3 4 5 6	1 2 3	1 2 3	1 2 3 4 5 6 7	1 2 3 4 5	1 2
7 8 9 10 11 12 13	4 5 6 7 8 9 10	4 5 6 7 8 9 10	8 9 10 11 12 13 14	6 7 8 9 10 11 12	3 4 5 6 7 8 9
14 15 16 17 18 19 20	11 12 13 14 15 16 17	11 12 13 14 15 16 17	15 16 17 18 19 20 21	13 14 15 16 17 18 19	10 11 12 13 14 15 16
21 22 23 24 25 26 27	18 19 20 21 22 23 24	18 19 20 **21** 22 23 24	22 23 24 25 26 27 28	20 21 22 23 24 25 26	17 18 19 20 21 22 23
28 29 30 21	25 26 27 28 29 30	25 26 27 28 29 30 31	29 30	27 28 29 30 31	24 25 26 27 28 29 30

July	August	September	October	November	December
S M T W TH F SA	S M T W TH F SA	S M T W TH F SA	S M T W TH F SA	S M T W TH F SA	S M T W TH F SA
1 2 3 4 5 6 7	1 2 3 4	1	1 2 3 4 5 6	1 2 3	1
8 9 10 11 12 13 14	5 6 7 8 9 10 11	2 3 4 5 6 7 8	7 8 9 10 11 12 13	4 5 6 7 8 9 10	2 3 4 5 6 7 8
15 16 17 18 19 20 21	12 13 14 15 16 17 18	9 10 11 12 13 14 15	14 15 16 17 18 19 20	11 12 13 14 15 16 17	9 10 11 12 13 14 15
22 23 24 25 26 27 28	19 20 21 22 23 24 25	16 17 18 19 20 21 **22**	21 22 23 24 25 26 27	18 19 20 21 22 23 24	16 17 18 19 20 21 22
29 30 31	26 27 28 29 30 31	23/30 24 25 26 27 28 29	28 29 30 31	25 26 27 28 29 30	23 24 / 30 31 25 26 27 28 29

Name _____ **Date** _____

Activity 4

On the map, find the equator. Find the **Antarctic Circle**.

Trace the Antarctic Circle. Circle one.

The Antarctic Circle is by the (North/South) Pole.

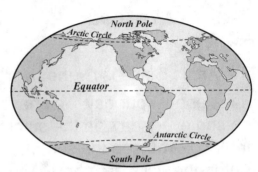

The Arctic Circle is not the same as the Antarctic Circle. One is north. One is south. When it is light in the Arctic Circle, it is dark in the Antarctic Circle. When it is dark in the Arctic Circle, it is light in the Antarctic Circle.

In the Antarctic Circle, the sun rises on September 22nd. It sets on March 20th. It is light all day. The sun never sets.

In the Antarctic Circle, the sun sets on March 21st. It is dark. It is dark for six months. The sun never rises.

Look at the calendar. Color the days it is light below the Antarctic Circle.

When it is dark in the Antarctic Circle, it is _____ in the Arctic Circle. (Circle the correct choice.)

A. dark   **B.** light   **C.** the same

January							February							March							April							May							June						
S	M	T	W	TH	F	SA	S	M	T	W	TH	F	SA	S	M	T	W	TH	F	SA	S	M	T	W	TH	F	SA	S	M	T	W	TH	F	SA	S	M	T	W	TH	F	SA
	1	2	3	4	5	6						1	2					1	2	3	1	2	3	4	5	6	7			1	2	3	4	5						1	2
7	8	9	10	11	12	13	4	5	6	7	8	9	10	4	5	6	7	8	9	10	8	9	10	11	12	13	14	6	7	8	9	10	11	12	3	4	5	6	7	8	9
14	15	16	17	18	19	20	11	12	13	14	15	16	17	11	12	13	14	15	16	17	15	16	17	18	19	20	21	13	14	15	16	17	18	19	10	11	12	13	14	15	16
21	22	23	24	25	26	27	18	19	20	21	22	23	24	18	19	20	21	22	23	24	22	23	24	25	26	27	28	20	21	22	23	24	25	26	17	18	19	20	21	22	23
28	29	30	21				25	26	27	28	29	30		25	26	27	28	29	30	31	29	30						27	28	29	30	31			24	25	26	27	28	29	30

July							August							September							October							November							December						
S	M	T	W	TH	F	SA	S	M	T	W	TH	F	SA	S	M	T	W	TH	F	SA	S	M	T	W	TH	F	SA	S	M	T	W	TH	F	SA	S	M	T	W	TH	F	SA
1	2	3	4	5	6	7			1	2	3		4							1	1	2	3	4	5	6				1	2	3							1
8	9	10	11	12	13	14	5	6	7	8	9	10	11	2	3	4	5	6	7	8	7	8	9	10	11	12	13	4	5	6	7	8	9	10	2	3	4	5	6	7	8
15	16	17	18	19	20	21	12	13	14	15	16	17	18	9	10	11	12	13	14	15	14	15	16	17	18	19	20	11	12	13	14	15	16	17	9	10	11	12	13	14	15
22	23	24	25	26	27	28	19	20	21	22	23	24	25	16	17	18	19	20	21	22	21	22	23	24	25	26	27	18	19	20	21	22	23	24	16	17	18	19	20	21	22
29	30	31					26	27	28	29	30	31		23/30	24	25	26	27	28	29	28	29	30	31				25	26	27	28	29	30		23 24 / 30 31		25	26	27	28	29

Name _____ **Date** _____

Activity 5

Earth spins on its **axis**. As Earth turns, different sides of Earth face the sun. One side has day. The other side has night.

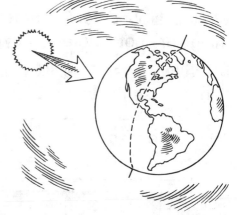

Look at the picture. Trace Earth's axis. Color the side of Earth where there is day. Shade in the side where there is night.

When something tilts, it leans. Earth **tilts** on its axis. It tilts as it goes around the sun. As Earth goes around the sun, different parts of Earth tilt to the sun. The parts that tilt toward the sun are warm. The days are long. It is summer. The parts that tilt away are cold. The days are short. It is winter.

Look at the picture. Put a box around the globe where it is summer at the North Pole and winter at the South Pole.

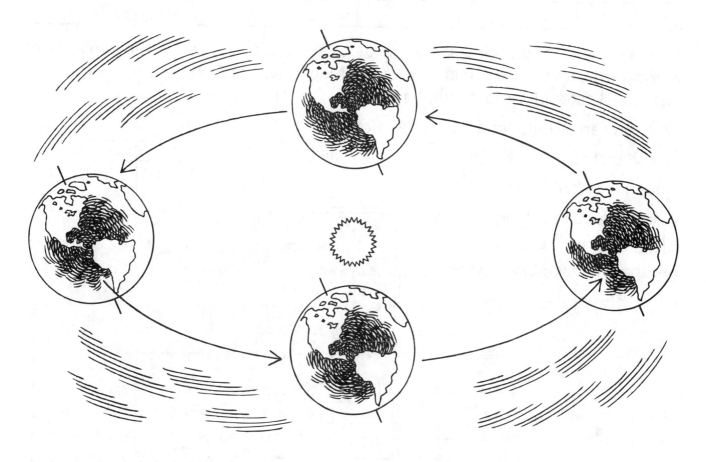

Name _____ **Date** _____

Activity 6

What is around you? Some things are natural. They are not man-made. Other things are not natural. They are man-made.

Make two lists. One list will be of natural things. One list will be of man-made things. Use the words below, as well as some of your own words.

| ocean | rain forest | bridge | playground |
| road | mountain | gulf | canal |

NATURAL	MAN-MADE
1.	1.
2.	2.
3.	3.
4.	4.
5.	5.

Donya was in Florida. She saw an alligator in the Everglades. The Everglades is a big **swamp**. A swamp is a wetland. Megan was in Florida, too. Megan saw an alligator in a zoo by the bay.

Who saw an alligator in a natural landform?

A. Donya   **B.** Megan

Find Florida on the map.

Which direction is Florida from where you live? _____

Are there any wetlands where you live? _____

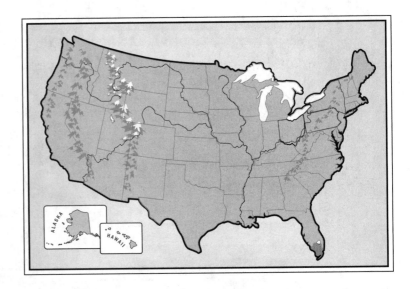

62

Name _____ **Date** _____

Activity 7

The world can change. It changes all the time. Some changes are natural.

A natural change might be

A. when a canal is dug

C. when crops are planted

B. when a volcano erupts

D. when a swamp is drained

Running water can cause a natural change. It erodes land. It can carve out canyons. A **canyon** is a valley with steep sides and a flat bottom.

The running water carries away dirt and rock. It carries it to standing water. Standing water does not flow. When the dirt is dumped, it is called **silt**.

Label the picture. Use the words below.

> flowing water   standing water   canyon   silt

Name some bodies of running water and standing water in your area.

_____

_____

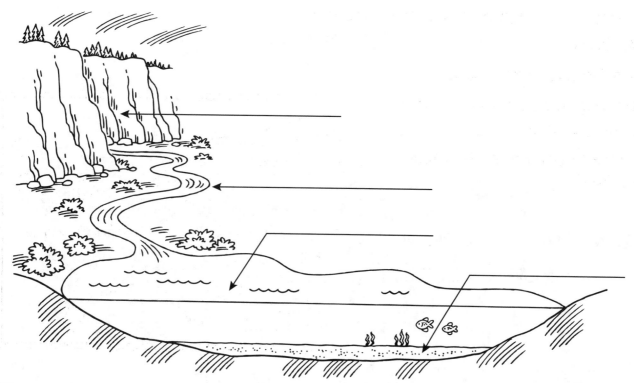

Where Animals and Plants Are Found

What I Need to Know

Vocabulary

- ecosystem
- food chain
- food web

About Animals and Plants

Animals and plants are linked. They are connected. They make up an ecosystem. Not all the ecosystems are the same. Different ecosystems have different plants. They have different animals.

You are part of an ecosystem. You are linked to animals. You are linked to plants. Different ecosystems are found all around the world.

What I Do

Read and complete each Activity. When you are done, you will know about a mammal that has a tongue as long as its body! You will also learn about a bird that helps crocodiles.

64

Name _____ **Date** _____

Activity 1

A Monarch butterfly lays eggs. The eggs hatch. Tiny caterpillars, or larva, hatch out. The caterpillars eat only one kind of plant. They only eat the milkweed plant. The milkweed plant has poison in it. Animals and bugs will not eat the plant. But the caterpillars do. The poison stays in the caterpillars.

The caterpillars change. They change into monarch butterflies. Animals will not eat the butterflies. Why not? The milkweed poison is in the butterflies!

The plant and the butterfly are linked. They are part of an **ecosystem**. In an ecosystem, plants and animals are linked. Not all the ecosystems are the same. You are part of an ecosystem too.

From the story, you can tell that

   A. all ecosystems are the same

   B. you are not part of an ecosystem

   C. there are different kinds of ecosystems

   D. plants and animals are not linked in an ecosystem

Circle the diagram that shows things linked together.

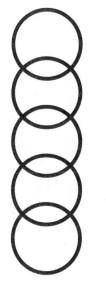

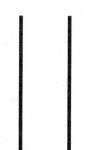

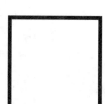

Name _____ **Date** _____

Activity 2

There is only one mammal that can fly. It is the bat. A mammal is warm-blooded. Bats live in many places. They live on every continent but one. They do not live on Antarctica.

All bats are not the same. Some are big. Some are small. Some eat different things. They are part of different ecosystems.

Most bats eat insects. If all the bats were gone, what might happen?

A. There would be more mammals.

B. Ecosystems would stay the same.

C. Many more insects would be bugging us.

D. Mammals would stop eating different things.

Why aren't bats in Antarctica?

A. It is too warm, and the insects are too big.

B. It is too cold, and all the insects are the same.

C. It is too cold, and there is nothing for them to eat.

D. It is too warm, and all the insects hide in the grass.

Find Antarctica on the map.
Is Antarctica north or south of the equator?_____

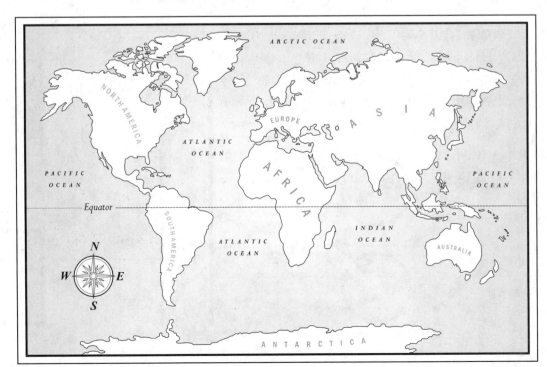

Name _____ **Date** _____

Activity 3

Think about how big you are. How much do you weigh? Now, think of two of you! Could you eat that much in one day? No way!

But some bats can. Some fruit bats live in Africa. They are part of an African ecosystem. It is a tropical forest ecosystem. These bats eat 2½ times their weight in fruit!

See how much a bat eats. Draw a box in the space below. This box shows how much a bat weighs.

Now, draw two and a half more boxes the same size as the first one. These boxes show how much of its weight a bat eats.

The bats fly from fruit to fruit. As they fly, they drop seeds. The seeds are from fruit. The seeds land on the ground. Later, the seeds grow. The bats are important. They help plants grow. They are an important part of the ecosystem.

Think about a monkey. Monkeys eat plants and fruit. How do bats help monkeys?

_____

_____

_____

_____

Name _____ **Date** _____

Activity 4

Bats need places to sleep. Bats need places to have their babies. Some bats live in caves. Some bats live in old barns. Some bats live in forests.

We need bats. But sometimes we make it hard for bats. We go into caves. We wake the bats when they need to sleep. We bother the bats when they have babies. Or, we knock down old barns. We chop down forests. The bats have no safe place to stay. By harming bats, we can harm an ecosystem.

From the story, you can tell that

   A. all bats live in caves   **C.** ecosystems can be harmed

   B. bats sleep all the time   **D.** bats do not need a safe place to stay

Bats sleep hanging upside down.

Can you sleep hanging upside down?

Some bats sip nectar. They go from flower to flower. They spread pollen from flower to flower. This helps flowers make seeds. A nectar bat has a long tongue. How long? As long as its body!

Draw a nectar bat with its tongue out in the box below.

Name _____ **Date** _____

Activity 5

A **food chain** shows links. It shows what eats what. Not all food chains are the same. Each ecosystem has different food chains. Fill in the blanks for the different food chains. The first one has been done for you. It shows how snakes eat birds. It shows that birds eat insects. The snake is higher up on the food chain.

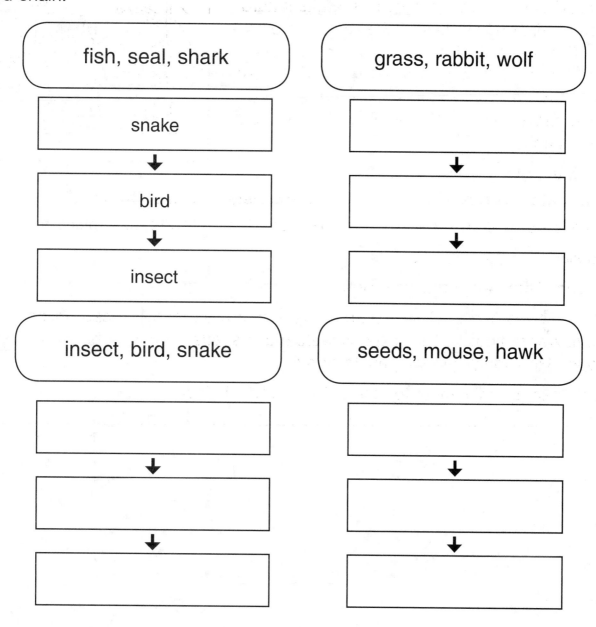

Which is higher on the food chain—a rabbit or a wolf? _____

Name _____ **Date** _____

Activity 6

A **food web** is made up of food chains. A food web shows how food chains are linked. Fill in the blanks. The blanks show a food web. The food web shows how animals and plants are linked in an ecosystem.

Use the words below to fill in the blanks.

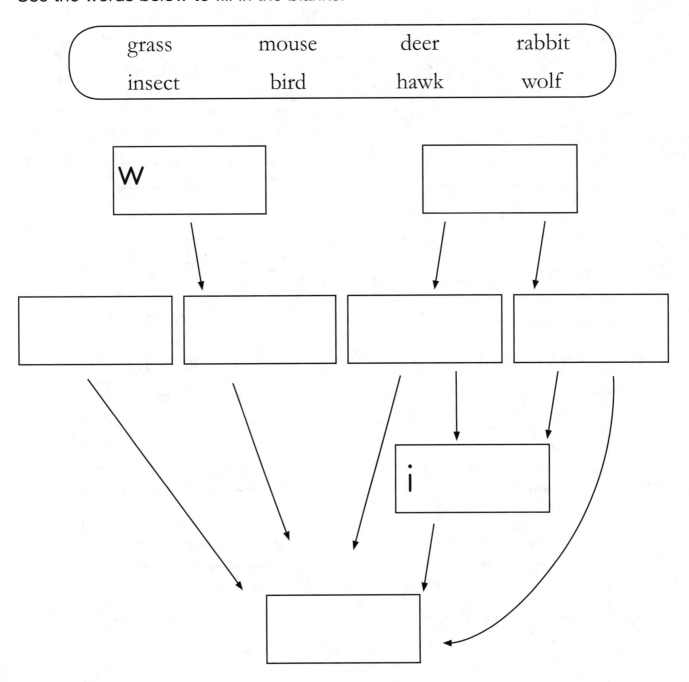

Name _____ **Date** _____

Activity 7

The Nile crocodile lives in the Nile River. It opens its mouth. A bird jumps in! The crocodile does not shut its mouth. It does not eat the bird. What is going on?

The bird is helping the crocodile. The bird is eating leeches in the crocodile's mouth. The leeches live in the Nile River. They get in the crocodile's mouth. They suck blood from the crocodile's gums. The crocodile cannot get them off. But the bird can! The bird eats the leeches! The crocodile is glad to get rid of the leeches. The bird is lucky to have a free dinner.

If it weren't for the crocodile, the bird would not be able to eat the leeches because

- **A.** the leeches suck blood
- **B.** the leeches live in water
- **C.** the leeches would get in the bird's mouth
- **D.** the leeches are not part of the ecosystem

On the map, find the Nile River.

The Nile River is on which continent? _____

The Nile River flows into which sea? _____

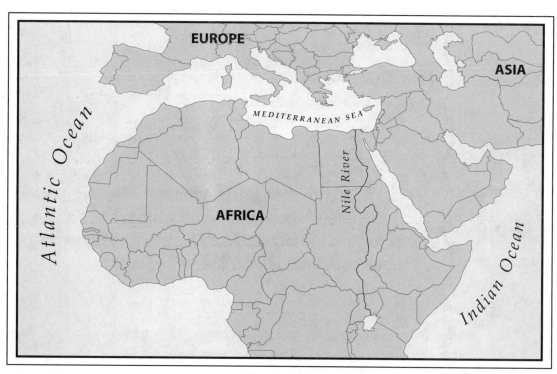

Where People Go

About Where People Go

People come. People go. They go to new places. They may stay. They may keep moving. Some people live in cities. They live near many other people. Why do people move? Why do they stay where they do? People go where they can live. They go where they can find food. They go where they can work. Our world can shape where people go. For example, many people live near rivers.

What I Need to Know

Vocabulary

- suburb

What I Do

Read and complete each Activity. When you are done, you will know where the world's biggest cities are, why it took longer to get to places long ago, and why one smoke jumper could not fight a fire.

Name _____ **Date** _____

Activity 1

Where do you live? Do you live in a city? Do you live in the country? Do you live in the **suburbs**? A suburb is a place. It is where people live. It is just outside a city or town.

Circle where you live: city   country   suburb

Write your address. _____

Where do people live today in the United States? Most people live in cities and suburbs. Show how many by coloring four of the boxes.

The colored boxes show how many people live in cities and suburbs. The box you did not color shows how many people live in the country.

Why do people live where they do? Think about work.   Think about stores. Think about hospitals.

_____

_____

_____

Make a list of some city jobs. Put a circle around the job if you know someone who does this job.

_____

_____

_____

_____

Name _____ **Date** _____

Activity 2

On the map, find Boston and Philadelphia. About how far away are they from each other?

A. 100 miles   **B.** 200 miles   **C.** 300 miles   **D.** 400 miles

1755 was long ago. How many years ago was 1755? _____

Here's how to figure it out:

Today's year:

_____

     – <u>1755</u>

In 1755, how long did it take to go from Boston to Philadelphia? It took one week. Why? (Pick two.)

A. Rain turned the roads to mud.

B. It was hard to find gas for cars.

C. People went by horseback or horse-drawn wagon.

D. People wanted to stop and see friends on the way.

Which city is farthest north?

_____

_____

Are the two cities on the West Coast or East Coast?

_____

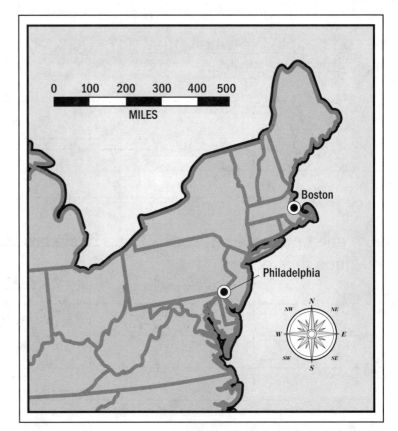

Name _____ **Date** _____

Activity 3

How long does it take to get from Boston to Philadelphia today? It does not take a week. You can drive. That takes 7½ hours. You can take a train. That takes 7 hours. You can fly. That takes 1½ hours.

Make a bar graph. The bar graph makes it easy to tell the difference in travel time.

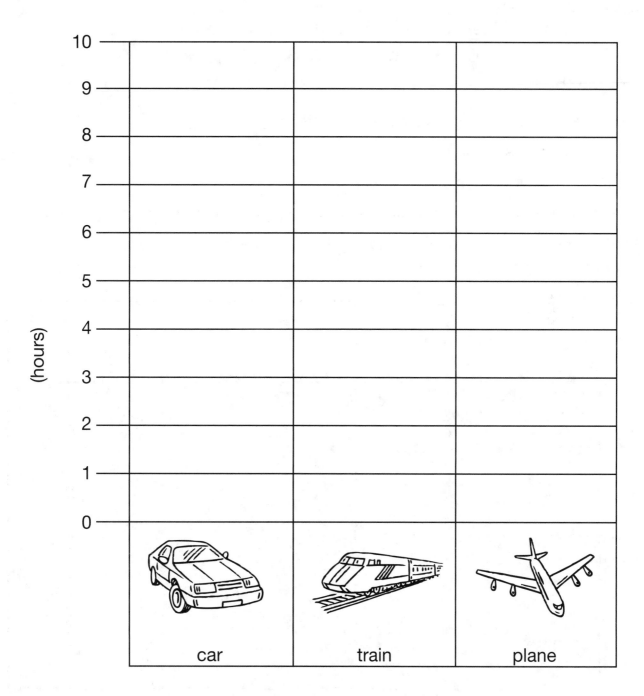

Name _____ **Date** _____

Activity 4

Some cities have lots of people, and some cities have very few people. Cities change. They get more people. Sometimes people move away. Find the eight big cities on the map. Write the name of the country each city is in on the map next to the city name. (These cities were the eight biggest cities in 2000.)

1. Tokyo, Japan

2. Mexico City, Mexico

3. New York City, United States

4. Sao Paulo, Brazil

5. Mumbai (Bombay), India

6. Kolkata (Calcutta), India

7. Shanghai, China

8. Buenos Aires, Argentina

How many of these eight cities are in Asia? _____

Which two cities are in North America? _____

Which two cities are in South America? _____

Which one of these cities is closest to where you live? _____

Do you think these cities were as big 100 years ago? Write one reason why or why not.

_____

_____

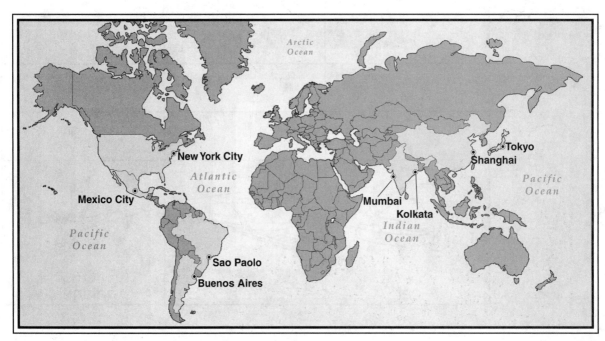

Name _____ **Date** _____

Activity 5

Smoke jumpers fight fires. Smoke jumpers put on parachutes and jump out of planes. They land near fires that are deep in the forest.

There was a fire in Alaska. It was where there were no roads. Smoke jumpers jumped. They were ready to fight the fire. But one smoke jumper could not! Why not? He landed on the wrong side of the river! He could not cross the deep, cold river. He could see the other smoke jumpers. He could see them fight the fire. He could see them work hard. But the one smoke jumper could only wait. He had to wait for the plane to pick him up after the other smoke jumpers had put out the fire!

From the story, you can tell that rivers

  A. are easy for people and animals to cross

  B. can stop people and animals from moving to new places

What do we build so we can get to a river's other side?

  A. dams

  B. bridges

Why aren't smoke jumpers needed in cities?_____

_____

Name _____ **Date** _____

Activity 6

People settle by rivers because they need water to drink. They need water to grow things. They can travel on the river. They can carry goods in boats and barges.

On the map, trace the rivers with a blue pencil or crayon.

Which state is the Yukon River in? _____

The Mississippi River empties into which gulf? _____

Which river starts in Colorado and runs through New Mexico and Texas? _____

Which river runs through Montana and North Dakota? _____

Which river starts in Pennsylvania? _____

Which river is closest to where you live? (The closest river may not be one of the ones listed above.)

_____

Name _____ **Date** _____

Activity 7

People ask questions. They ask questions to find out about people and how they live.

Make tally marks for how many in your class.

SIBLINGS	
0	
1	
2	
3	
4	
5	

PETS	
dog	
cat	
fish	
other	

What other questions could you ask about your class?

1. _____
_____
_____
_____

2. _____
_____
_____
_____

TIMES MOVED TO NEW CITY	
0	
1	
2	
3	
4	

GET TO SCHOOL	
walk	
bus	
car ride	
train or subway	

3. _____
_____
_____
_____

In Saudi Arabia, boys and girls have to go to different schools. Do boys and girls go to separate schools in your country?_____

Find and label Saudi Arabia on the map.

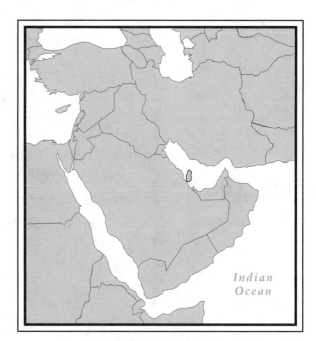

Indian Ocean

People Patterns

About People Patterns

You have a culture. You are part of a culture. What is a culture? How do we know what our culture is? Culture is learned. It is how we talk, our language, and what we believe. It is our religion, how we dress, how we treat one another, and how we work.

All over the world, people have different cultures. The different cultures make up patterns. As people move, parts of new and old cultures are shared. New patterns are taking shape.

What I Need to Know

Vocabulary

- culture

What I Do

Read and complete each Activity. When you are done, you will know where peanuts first came from, a place where you stick out your tongue to say "hi," and why some houses got bigger.

Name _____   **Date** _____

Activity 1

Stick out your tongue! Were you rude? Did you forget your manners?

Stick out your tongue! Were you saying "hi"? Were you showing that you liked someone?

Stick out your tongue! Were you showing that you were embarrassed?

All people do not do things the same. They do things differently. Each group of people is special. They have ways of doing things. These things add up to a people's **culture**. Culture is learned. Our culture is how we live. It is what we eat, what we believe, and how we do things.

If you stick out your tongue, what are you? In the United States, you are rude. If you are an Aborigine in Australia, you are not rude. You are saying "hi." You are showing that you are glad to see someone. If you were in one part of China, it is a sign of embarrassment.

Find the United States on the map.

Find Australia on the map.

Find China on the map.

Circle the country that is a whole continent.

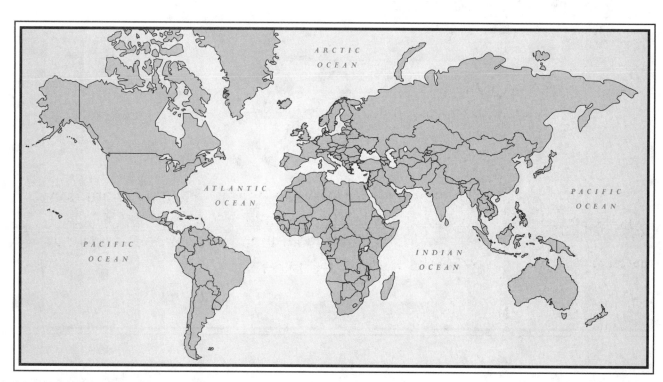

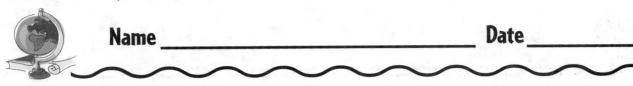

Name _____ **Date** _____

Activity 2

What language or languages do you speak?

We have a language. It is part of our culture. How many languages are there? A lot! More than 2,800! What languages are spoken the most? The most spoken languages are (in order):

	ONE COUNTRY WHERE SPOKEN
1. Mandarin Chinese	China
2. Spanish	Mexico
3. English	England
4. Hindi	India
5. Portuguese	Portugal

SAY, *HI.*	ONE COUNTRY WHERE SPOKEN
Swahili: *jambo*	Kenya
SAY *GOOD-BYE.*	
Dutch: *dag*	Netherlands
SAY *THANK-YOU.*	
Swedish: *tack tack*	Sweden

Practice speaking other languages with a partner.

On the map, find and write the names of the countries above.

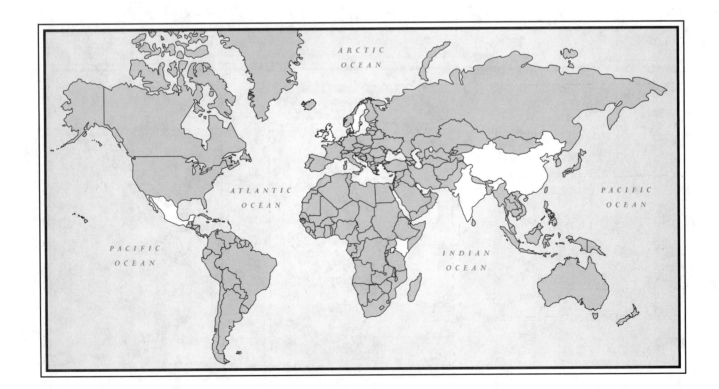

Name _____ **Date** _____

Activity 3

What we eat is part of our culture. Different cultures eat different foods.

Do you like peanut butter?_____

Do you like fries? _____

Many people think of these foods as "American." Today peanut butter is part of the American food culture. So are fries. But they were not always!

Long ago, peanuts were only in South America. Potatoes were only in South America. Explorers from Europe brought these foods home. Explorers brought new foods to the new countries. Food cultures changed all around the world.

Pick two foods from each continent. Draw the food on the continent it first came from.

Asia	
lemon	rice
peach	wheat

Africa	
coffee	melon
okra	yam

South America	
corn	pineapple
tomato	chocolate

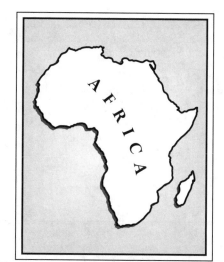

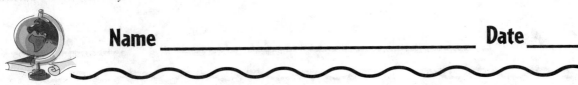

Name _____ **Date** _____

Activity 4

In some cultures, people eat with chopsticks. In some cultures, people eat with silverware. They eat with spoons, knives, and forks. In other cultures, people eat with their hands.

How do you eat? Draw a circle around what you use to eat.

On the map, find Vietnam, France, and Eritrea.

In Vietnam, many people use chopsticks.

In France, many people use silverware.

In Eritrea, many people use their hands.

On which continent is Vietnam? _____

On which continent is France? _____

On which continent is Eritrea?_____

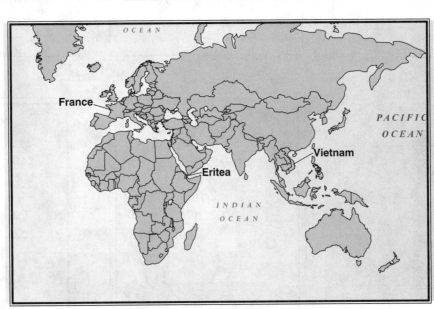

Do you mind your manners? In Eritrea it is bad manners to eat with one's left hand. One should eat with one's right hand.

Name _____ **Date** _____

Activity 5

People live in houses. Are all houses the same? No, the houses are not the same. They are different in different places. Different culture groups build different houses.

How are the houses different? One difference is how they are built. They are built with different materials. Some houses are made of wood. Some houses are made of rock. Some houses are made of earth.

The Great Plains in the United States are flat. They are grassy. They have few trees. Long ago, Native Americans lived in teepees. The teepees could be taken down. They could be moved. The Native Americans used dogs. The dogs helped carry the teepees.

The teepees were most likely made of

A. wood   **B.** rock   **C.** skins   **D.** earth

Something happened. The teepees got bigger. Why? There was a new animal. Spanish explorers brought it. The animal was strong. It could carry bigger teepees.

What was the animal?

A. a cat   **B.** a deer   **C.** a horse   **D.** a buffalo

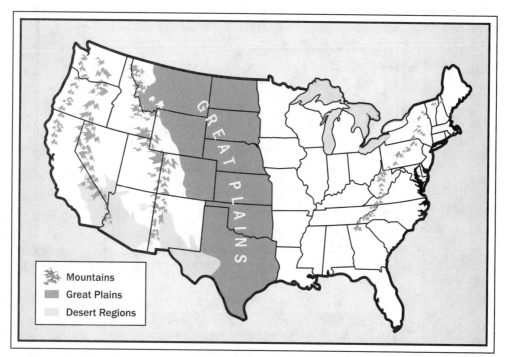

Mountains
Great Plains
Desert Regions

Name _____ **Date** _____

Activity 6

You go to school to learn to read, write, do math, and many other skills. Going to school is part of your culture.

In Pakistan, children do not have to go to school as long as you do. Children only have to go to school until they are nine years old. The classes are free, but they are large. Often, a class will have 40 children. How many children are in your class?

Some children are not sent to school in Pakistan. Why might parents in Pakistan and other countries not send children to school?

A. They want them to learn to read.   **C.** They need them to help at home.

B. They want them to play all day.   **D.** They live close to the schools.

Many girls carry water. They carry water to their homes. The water is for cooking, drinking, and washing.

All around the world, more girls go to school when

A. water is nearby   **B.** water is far away

Find and color Pakistan on the map below.

Pakistan is on which continent? _____

Pakistan borders which ocean? _____

Is Pakistan north or south of the equator?

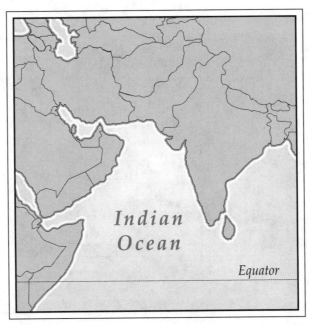

Name _____ **Date** _____

Activity 7

All around the world, people wear different kinds of clothes. What we wear is part of our culture. Some fishermen in Ireland wore sweaters. The sweaters were knitted. They were wool. The wool came from sheep. The sheep were raised in Ireland.

Why were these sweaters part of the fisherman's culture? The sheep wool was warm and oily. The oily sheep wool helped make the sweaters waterproof!

From the story, you can tell that

A. all sweaters are knitted

C. fishermen today wear raincoats to stay dry

B. sweaters must be waterproof

D. wool sweaters were part of some people's culture

Find and label Ireland on the map.

Which continent is it part of? _____

Circle two items below that are part of your clothes culture.

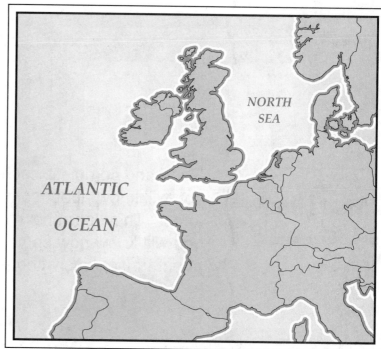

Buying and Selling Around the World

Vocabulary

- capital
- barge
- port

About Buying and Selling

All over the world, people trade. They buy goods and sell goods. Sometimes the goods are sold and sent far away. You may eat foods not grown in your country. They were grown far away. Goods may be put together in your state. The goods are then sold far away.

The goods are moved in different ways. Some goods are carried in trucks. Some goods are carried in planes. Some goods are carried on barges and ships. In some places, goods are carried on the backs of bicycles.

What I Do

Read and complete each Activity. When you are done, you will know about some children who live in a rain forest. They learn how to build fires and make grass huts. You will know how some things are moved. You will know about traffic jams without cars.

Name _____ **Date** _____

Activity 1

Joy lives in Delaware. Delaware is a state. It is part of the United States. Joy and her Dad get in a car. They drive to a store. They buy milk. Joy drinks milk. They buy coffee. Joy's dad drinks coffee.

Milk comes from cows. Cows are raised on a dairy farm. The dairy farm is in Wisconsin. Wisconsin is a state. It is part of the United States. Coffee comes from a plant. It is made from coffee plant beans. The plants do not grow in the United States. Some coffee plants grow in Costa Rica. The coffee Joy's dad got was from Costa Rica.

From the story, you can tell that

A. milk comes from a plant

C. sometimes food is grown in faraway places

B. coffee is grown on a dairy farm

D. Joy will drink coffee when she goes to Wisconsin

On the map on page 172, find Delaware, Wisconsin, and Costa Rica.

How do you think the milk and the coffee got to Delaware? _____

_____

_____

_____

_____

Name _____ **Date** _____

Activity 2

Dhaka is a city. It is a capital. A capital city is where the government meets. It is where the government offices are. All countries have capitals. Dhaka is the capital of Bangladesh. Many people live in the city. Many people do not have cars. How do the people get about? How do they get to the store?

They use rickshas. A ricksha is a kind of taxi. It is not a car. It does not use gas. How does it go? People make it go. Many of the rickshas in Dhaka are like bikes. They have carts on them. The carts have seats. People sit in the carts. The driver pedals the bike to make it go. In Dhaka there are more than 300,000 rickshas. There are traffic jams. The traffic is made up of rickshas!

Is the city you live in a capital?

What is the name of your country's capital?

What is the name of your state's capital?

Does Dhaka or your city have more rickshas?

People might use rickshas because

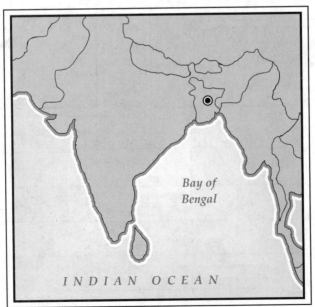

  A. rickshas use gas

  B. the stores are nearby

  C. cars cost too much money

  D. people can walk faster than a bike can go

On the map, find and label Dhaka and Bangladesh.

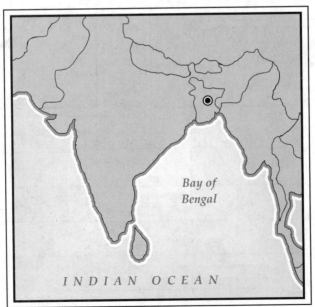

Bay of Bengal

INDIAN OCEAN

BANGLADESH

Name _____

Date _____

Activity 3

We use iron ore. We use it to make steel. Steel is strong. We use it to make many things. Think of three things made with steel.

1. _____
2. _____
3. _____

How do we get iron ore? We mine it. We dig it out of the ground. A lot of iron ore is mined in Minnesota. It is mined in the Mesabi Range. The iron ore is dug out of the ground. Then it is sold around the world. It is sold to places where steel is made.

Think about the iron ore. Think about how it goes to places where steel is made.

Would taking the iron ore by ricksha be a good way to move it? _____

Why or why not? _____

How might the iron ore be moved? _____

Find and label Minnesota on the map. Circle the Mesabi Range.

Which direction is Minnesota from where you live? _____

If there is one, name a state between your state and Minnesota. _____

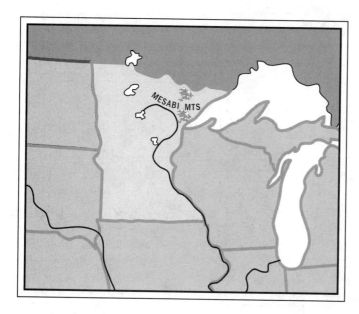

Name _____ **Date** _____

Activity 4

Some Minnesota iron ore is put on barges. A **barge** is a long, flat ship. Some barges go down the Mississippi River. Other barges are loaded in Duluth. Duluth is a port. A **port** is a harbor. It is a place where ships can load and unload.

Duluth is a busy port. It is the busiest freshwater port in the United States. Where does the iron go from Duluth? It goes to the Atlantic Ocean! How? It goes through the Great Lakes. It goes down the St. Lawrence River.

Find Duluth on the map. Trace a line from Duluth to the Atlantic Ocean.

The line should go through four Great Lakes. Which Great Lake does your line not go through?

  A. Lake Erie   **B.** Lake Ontario   **C.** Lake Michigan   **D.** Lake Superior

The Saint Lawrence River flows through which country?

  A. Mexico   **B.** Canada

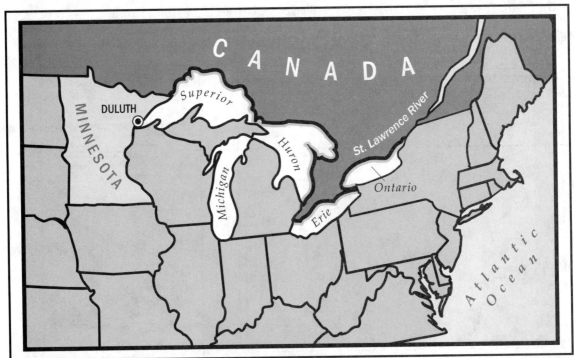

Name _____ **Date** _____

Activity 5

Think about where you live. Think about your state. What goods are grown in your state? Or, what goods are made in your state? List five things grown or made in your state.

1. _____
2. _____
3. _____
4. _____
5. _____

Sketch a map of your state. Show on your map the areas where the goods listed are grown or made. Use the map below to help you make your own map.

Sample Map:

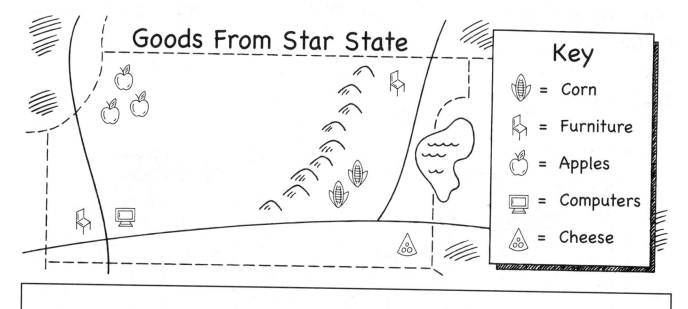

Goods From Star State

Key

= Corn

= Furniture

= Apples

= Computers

= Cheese

Name _____ **Date** _____

Activity 6

Think about the grocery store.

What is most likely next to apples: oranges or bread? _____

What is most likely next to milk: cheese or canned beans?_____

What is most likely next to dog food: pizza or cat food? _____

In some ways, cities are like grocery stores. Some stores or places are more likely to be near each other. Government offices are close together. Stores are close together. Houses are close together.

Look at the map. There are five empty places. Write the name of one of the places listed below in each space. Use each place only once.

1. house   **2.** grocery store   **3.** doctor's office   **4.** bakery   **5.** shoe store

Why would a gas station be near a busy road?_____

_____

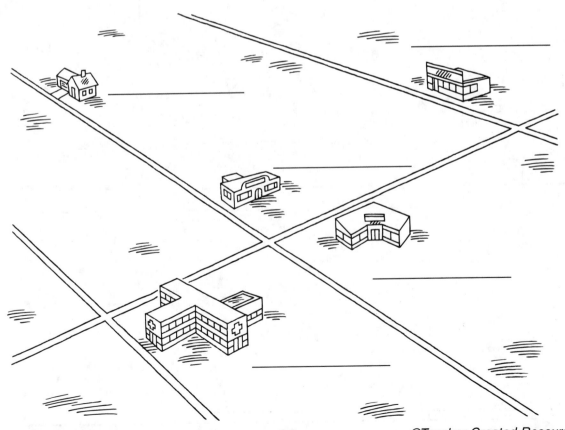

Name _____ **Date** _____

Activity 7

Aswa is a Mbuti pygmy. Mbuti pygmies live in rain forests. They live where there are very few roads. They live in the Democratic Republic of Congo.

How big are pygmies? An average man is 4 feet 3 inches (130 cm) tall. An average woman is 4 feet (122 cm).

The men hunt for wild animals. They use poisoned arrows.

The women look for roots, for berries, and wild plants.

The young children learn how to build fires. They learn how to make grass huts.

What do you learn to do?_____

_____

_____

Find the and label Democratic Republic of Congo on the map (use **DRC**).

On which continent is the Democratic Republic of Congo? _____

Which ocean borders the Democratic Republic of Congo? _____

Where People Settle

What I Need to Know

Vocabulary

- fertile
- natural resource

About Where People Settle

People live in many places. They settle all around the world. People use the land around them in different ways. In some places, land is used for growing food. In other places, land is used for cities.

Places where people settle may change. They can grow. If factories are built, workers will come. The workers will bring their families. Stores and schools will be needed for the workers' families. Many houses may be in one area. Many businesses may be near big roads.

What I Do

Read and complete each Activity. When you are done, you will know about a lake that is not filled with water, about some houses that are under the ground, and about a city that is very old.

Name _____ **Date** _____

Activity 1

Find Tunisia on the map. Tunisia is in

A. East Africa **B.** West Africa **C.** North Africa **D.** South Africa

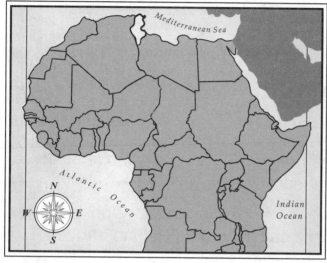

Some people in Tunisia live under the ground. Their homes have several rooms. One room is for sleeping. One room is for eating. One room is for storage. One room is for animals. There is a pipe in one ceiling. Food for animals is put down the pipe.

The homes keep the people safe. They are safe from sand. They are safe from wind. They are safe from wild animals. In the day, they are safe from the hot sun. In the night, they are safe from the cold air.

Most likely, the people who live under the ground in Tunisia

A. live in Tunis, the largest city **C.** live near the lake Shatt al Jarid

B. live near the Mediterranean Sea **D.** live in the desert part of Tunisia

Name _____ **Date** _____

Activity 2

Today, people go to Tunisia to see what is left of a city. The city is old. It is close to Tunis. It is over 3,000 years old. It is called Carthage.

Carthage was a strong city. It was a sea power. It had lots of ships.

Most likely Carthage was a sea power because

  A. it was by the Sahara Desert

  B. it was by the Atlas Mountains

  C. it was by the border of Algeria

  D. it was by the Mediterranean Sea

Long ago, Carthage was overthrown. It lost its power. Who overthrew it? The Romans overthrew it. The Romans came from Italy. Find and label Italy on the map. Trace a line from Italy to Carthage.

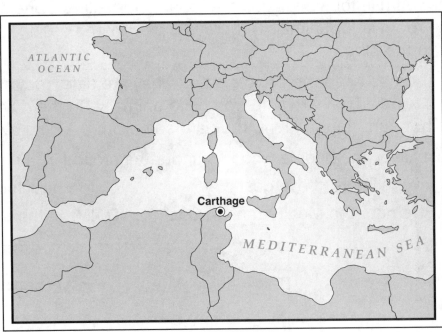

How old is the city you live in or are near to? _____

What do people today come to see in your city? _____

What people or country had power over your city long ago? _____

Name _____ **Date** _____

Activity 3

Long ago, there were no cities. People needed water. They needed food. They settled near water. They settled where the land was **fertile**. When something is fertile, it can grow things. People grew food on the fertile land. They watered their crops.

People began to grow enough food to trade. Then, not everyone had to grow food. Some people made things they could trade for food. People came together to trade and cities started to grow.

Damascus is an old city in Syria. People have lived in Damascus for a long time. It is the oldest existing city. It is the oldest city in the world that people still live in.

From the story, you can tell that

  A. cities began after people began to grow a lot of food

  B. cities began before people began to grow a lot of food

On the map, find and label Damascus and Syria.

Which continent is Syria on? _____

Is Syria north or south of the equator? _____

Equator

Name _____ **Date** _____

Activity 4

There were two towns. The towns were about the same size. Then something was built. One town got bigger. One town got smaller.

What might have been built?

A. a big highway that went by both towns

B. a big highway that only went by one town

C. a big highway that did not go by the towns

Some businesses start up faster than others. What business would most likely not start as fast as the others by a highway?

A. a shoe store

B. a gas station

C. a fast-food restaurant

D. a store for truck drivers

A factory is built. Workers come. Workers need homes and their children need schools. They need places to buy things.

A new factory may mean

A. many new jobs only in the factory

B. many new jobs only out of the factory

C. many new jobs in and out of the factory

Which town would most likely have the most pizza places?

A. a town with one factory

B. a town with five factories

Think about your city. Is it growing or getting smaller? List two reasons why it is growing or getting smaller.

1. _____

_____

2. _____

_____

Name _____ **Date** _____

Activity 5

Nan lives in La Brea. La Brea is a town in the country of Trinidad and Tobago. It is on the island of Trinidad. It is in the south. Near La Brea is a lake. The lake is not filled with water. It is filled with natural pitch. Pitch is a black, sticky tar. The tar is used for surfacing roads. Long ago, explorers used the tar on their ships. The tar kept the ship from leaking.

This lake is the world's largest single supply of natural pitch. It is a **natural resource**. A resource is a supply of something. It takes care of a need. A natural resource is found in nature. It is not man-made.

From the story, you can tell that

  A. there are not any water lakes in Trinidad

  B. one of Trinidad and Tobago's natural resources is pitch

  C. pitch is the only natural resource in the world

  D. some natural resources can be made in factories

On the map, find Trinidad and Tobago. Which sea and ocean surround Trinidad and Tobago?

  A. Caribbean Sea and Pacific Ocean

  B. Caribbean Sea and Atlantic Ocean

  C. Mediterranean Sea and Pacific Ocean

  D. Mediterranean Sea and Atlantic Ocean

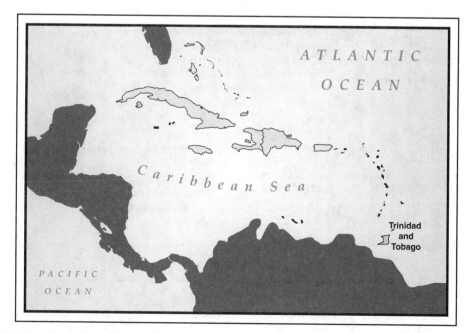

Name _____ **Date** _____

Activity 6

Fertile land is a natural resource. Water is a natural resource. Fertile land is often around rivers. Why? Sometimes rivers will flood. The rivers leave rich soil. The rich soil is fertile. Crops grow well in fertile soil.

Write *true* or *false* by each sentence. Use the map to help you find the answers.

_____ The Nile River is in Africa.

_____ The Amazon River is in Europe.

_____ The Huang Ho (Yellow) River is in Asia.

_____ The Ganges River is in South America.

_____ The Mississippi River is west of the Rio Grande.

_____ The Danube River is in Europe.

Most likely, some of the first cities _____ around these rivers.

A. grew up   **B.** did not grow up

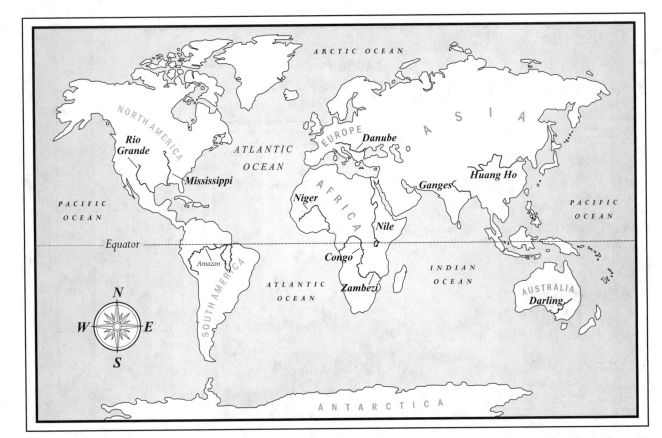

Name _____ **Date** _____

Activity 7

Make a line graph of the population of Tell City using the information in the chart. Put dots on the grid where the year and population number meet. Then connect the dots with a line.

TELL CITY POPULATION	
1850	5,000
1900	20,000
1950	25,000
2000	50,000

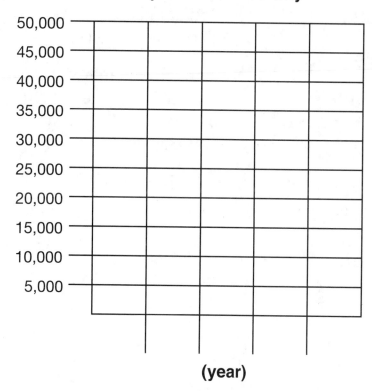

Population of Tell City

(year)

Two big things happened in Tell City. A railroad was built. The city got bigger. Later, many factories were built. The factories built computers, TVs, and cell phones. People came to work in the factories.

What years was the railroad most likely built?

A. 1850 to 1900   **B.** 1900 to 1950   **C.** 1950 to 2000

What years were the factories most likely built?

A. 1850 to 1900   **B.** 1900 to 1950   **C.** 1950 to 2000

How Earth Is Divided Up

What I Need to Know

Vocabulary

- country
- states
- Washington, D.C.
- county

About How Earth Is Divided Up

There is only one Earth but it has many parts. It is made up of many countries. Each country is different. Some countries are old. Some countries are young. Each country has a government. The government makes rules. The government meets in the country's capital city.

One country may have many parts. It may be made up of states. The states may have many parts too. States may be divided into counties. Cities and towns are in different counties.

What I Do

Read and complete each Activity. When you are done, you will know about a place where blind beetles live, an animal that can turn its ears in all directions, and where the capital of the United States is.

Name _____ **Date** _____

Activity 1

The United States is one **country**. It is made up of **states**. There are 50 states. The United States was not always a country. Before, it was made up of the Thirteen Colonies. The colonies belonged to England. The colonies broke away from England. They became states. Each state has a birthday. It is the day the state became one of the United States.

Look at the original states' birthdays. On the map, write the order each state became one of the United States. Delaware, the first state, has been done for you.

	DAY BECAME A STATE	NUMBER
Delaware	December 7, 1787	1
Pennsylvania	December 12, 1787	2
New Jersey	December 18, 1787	3
Georgia	January 2, 1788	4
Connecticut	January 9, 1788	5
Massachusetts	February 6, 1788	6
Maryland	April 28, 1788	7
South Carolina	May 23, 1788	8
New Hampshire	June 21, 1788	9
Virginia	June 25, 1788	10
New York	July 26, 1788	11
North Carolina	November 21, 1789	12
Rhode Island	May 29, 1790	13

When is your birthday?_____

Name _____ **Date** _____

Activity 2

On the map, find the states. Write the order each state became one of the United States.

	DAY BECAME A STATE	NUMBER
Tennessee	June 1, 1796	16
Louisiana	April 30, 1812	18
Illinois	December 3, 1818	21
Texas	December 29, 1845	28
Oregon	February 14, 1859	33
Nebraska	March 1, 1867	37
South Dakota	November 2, 1889	40
Wyoming	July 10, 1890	44
Hawaii	August 21, 1959	50

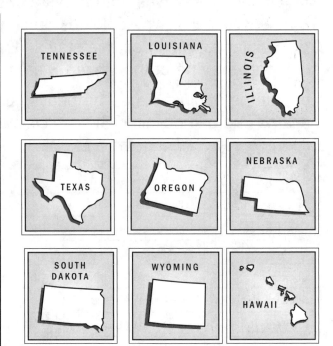

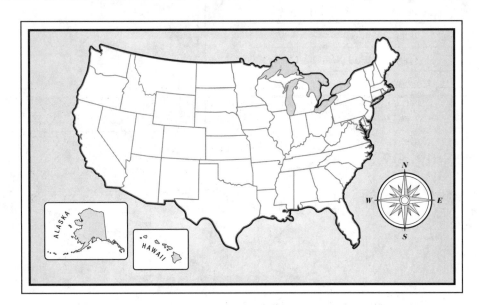

What is your state's number? _____

What is your state's birthday? _____

Each state has a state flag. On another sheet of paper, sketch your state's flag.

Name _____ **Date** _____

Activity 3

Each state has a capital. The United States has a capital, too. **Washington, D.C.** is the country's capital. The national government meets in Washington, D.C. What does the *DC* stand for? It stands for *District of Columbia*.

Find Washington, D.C. on the map.

Find these state capitals:

Olympia (Washington State)

Montgomery (Alabama)

Madison (Wisconsin)

Albany (New York)

Sacramento (California)

Austin (Texas)

Charleston (West Virginia)

Is Washington, D.C. the capital of Washington State?

_____

Which Washington is on the West Coast?

A. Washington State   **B.** Washington, D.C.

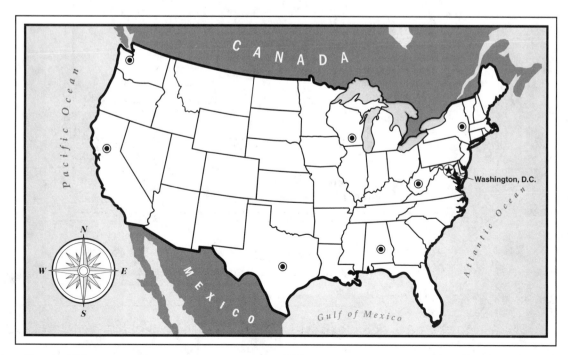

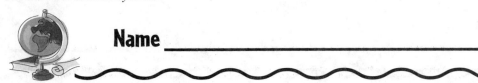

Name _____ **Date** _____

Activity 4

The president lives in Washington, D.C. The president leads the country. The president lives in the White House.

The Congress meets in Washington, D.C. The Congress makes laws and rules for the whole country. The Congress meets in the Capitol Building.

The Supreme Court meets in Washington, D.C. The Supreme Court is the highest court in the land. It says if laws are fair. It meets in the Supreme Court Building.

Use the map to answer the questions.

Which river flows past Washington, D.C.? _____

Who meets east of the Washington Monument?

  A. the Congress   **B.** the president

Which direction is the Lincoln Monument from the White House?

  A. northeast   **C.** southeast

  B. northwest   **D.** southwest

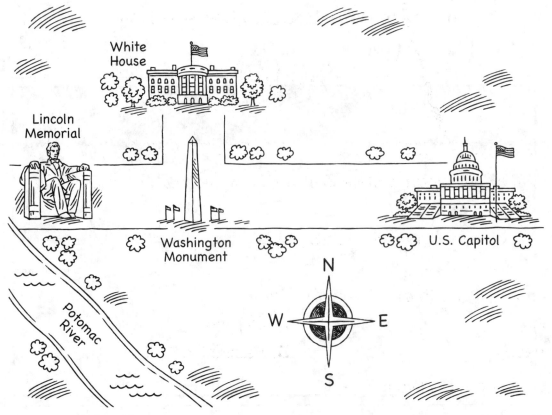

Name _____   **Date** _____

Activity 5

The United States is made up of states. What is a state made up of? A state is made up of counties.

The word **county** is almost like the word *country*. What letter changes the word county to country?

Look at the map of Washington State.

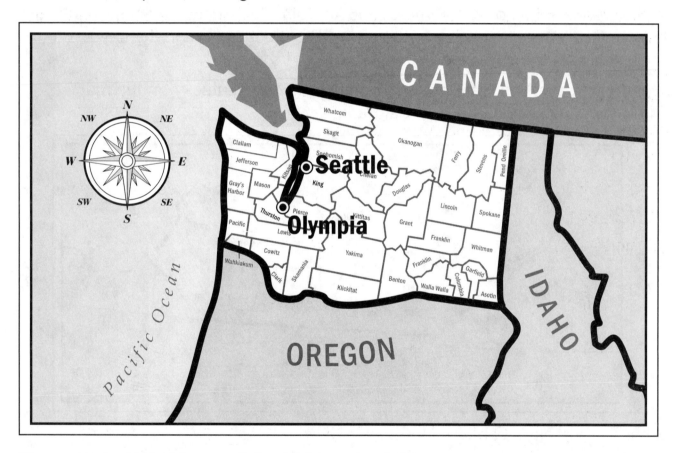

The capital of Washington State is Olympia. Which county is Olympia in?

_____

Seattle is a big city in Washington State. Which county is Seattle in?

_____

Which country is north of Washington State?

  A. Idaho   **B.** Oregon

  C. Canada   **D.** Pacific Ocean

Which county do you live in?_____

Name _____ **Date** _____

Activity 6

Some parks are city parks. Some parks are county parks. Some parks are state parks. Some parks are national parks.

The city pays for city parks. The county pays for county parks. The state pays for state parks. The national government pays for the national parks.

Mammoth Cave is a national park. Mammoth Cave is one of the biggest caves in the world. It has over 190 miles (306 km) of mapped passages. It has five levels. Fish without eyes live in the cave. Blind beetles live in the cave. Blind crickets live in the cave, too.

Mammoth Cave National Park is in Kentucky. Find Kentucky on the map. Circle the Mammoth Cave National Park.

What is Kentucky's capital?

A. Lexington   **B.** Frankfurt   **C.** Louisville   **D.** Bowling Green

It is always the same temperature in Mammoth Cave. It is 54°F (12°C). Why is this so? _____

_____

Why do you think so many animals are blind in Mammoth Cave? _____

_____

List some parks near you. Are they city, county, state, or national parks?

_____

Name _____ **Date** _____

Activity 7

How many countries are in the world? There are a lot! There are over 190 countries. Some countries are big. Some are small. Some countries have more people than others. Some countries are old. Some are new.

Are there more than or fewer than 150 countries in the world?

_____

Kenya is a country. Its first birthday was in 1963. Before that it was a colony. It belonged to England. The United States once belonged to England, too.

Is your country older or younger than Kenya?

_____

Lions are big cats. Lions can turn their ears from side to side. This helps them hear sounds from all directions. Lions can hear prey that is more than 1 mile (2 km) away!

Do lions live in your country? _____

Find and color Kenya and England on the map.

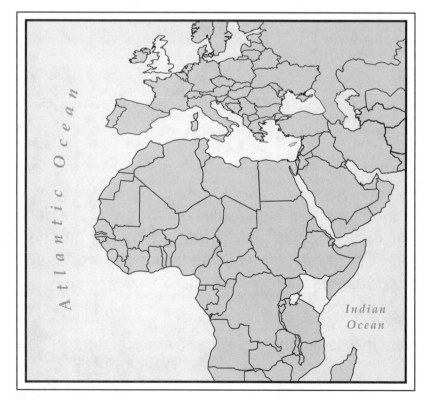

How People Shape Earth's Surface

What I Need to Know

Vocabulary

- oxygen
- carbon dioxide

About People Shaping Earth

Earth has four parts: air, water, land, and living things. Plants, animals, and people are all living things.

The parts are connected. People need all four parts. Sometimes, a change in one part may lead to changes in other parts. Some changes are natural. They are caused in nature. Other changes are man-made. The changes shape Earth. The new shape may mean that people may have to change how they live. The new shape may mean that people may have to change what they do.

What I Do

Read and complete each Activity. When you are done, you will know about big boats that are on dry ground. You will know about the fastest flying bird in the world, and a plant that has been grown for over 7,000 years.

Name _____   **Date** _____

Activity 1

Many big boats sit on the ground. They are not in the water. They are on the bottom of a sea. But they are on dry ground! How can this be?

The Aral Sea is a big sea between two countries.

Which two countries is the lake between?

 A. Kyrgyzstan and Tajikistan

 B. Kazakhstan and Uzbekistan

 C. Kazakhstan and Afghanistan

 D. Uzbekistan and Turkmenistan

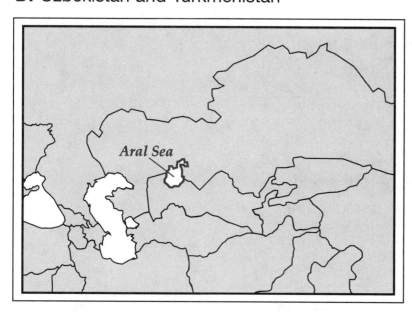

The Aral Sea is getting smaller. It is shrinking. It is almost half gone. Big boats are stuck. They are stuck on the dry ground.

Why might the Aral Sea be shrinking?

 A. More fish are being eaten.

 B. It is raining all the time.

 C. People are drinking more water.

 D. Not as much river water runs into the lake.

Is the Aral Sea north or south of the equator?_____

Name _____ **Date** _____

Activity 2

The Aral Sea is shrinking quickly. Water from rivers used to run into the Aral Sea. The water kept the sea full. The rivers do not flow just in Kazakhstan and Uzbekistan. They flow through other countries too.

All the countries use the water. They use the water to grow crops. One big crop is cotton. Now, less river water gets to the Aral Sea. The river water is used up. More lake water is used too. It is used for crops. It is used to grow cotton.

Why is there less water in the Aral Sea?

 A. Countries are growing less cotton.

 B. More river water is feeding the lake.

 C. River and lake water is being used for crops.

 D. The Aral Sea is flowing through other countries.

From the story, you can tell that

 A. water does not have to be shared

 B. people need to stop growing crops

 C. how we use water can change our world

 D. cotton is a crop that does not need water

On which continent are Kazakhstan and Uzbekistan? _____

Name _____ **Date** _____

Activity 3

Look at the charts.

Animals seen by Dora and Steve in one week:

Chart A

ANIMAL	NUMBER
Deer	8
Hawks	4
Pigeons	4
Cats	1
Rats	1
Dogs	2

Chart B

ANIMAL	NUMBER
Deer	0
Hawks	1
Pigeons	35
Cats	9
Rats	2
Dogs	5

Which chart is most likely a chart made in a city? _____

Why would one see more deer in the country? _____

_____

Make a chart. Keep track of how many animals you see in a day or a week.
How many different kinds do you think you will see? What animal do you think
you will see the most?

Animals I saw in one week

ANIMAL	NUMBER

Name _____ **Date** _____

Activity 4

Think about where you live and what it was like in the past. Can you think of any animals that lived in your area long ago? List three animals. Draw a picture of one in the box below.

1. _____

2. _____

3. _____

Circle the animals if they still live in your area today.

Animals go away for many reasons. What answer is not a reason why animals might go away?

A. Houses are built where the animals lived.

B. The land is plowed so crops can be planted.

C. A park is made for animals to live in the wild.

D. Roads stop the animals from getting to clean water.

Name _____ **Date** _____

Activity 5

Think like a detective. The peregrine falcon is the fastest bird in the world.
It dives at speeds over 200 miles (322 km) per hour! The peregrine falcon
catches other birds.

Falcons are not city birds. But people brought some falcons to big cities. They
let the birds go.

Why? Falcons were used to

  A. scare people

  B. pick up paper scraps

  C. nest on the buildings

  D. keep the number of pigeons down

People brought some falcons to airports. They let the birds go.

Why? Falcons were used to

  A. show people the way to the city

  B. keep the people on the planes happy

  C. test how fast the planes were going

  D. keep the runways and planes free of pest birds

Can you run as fast as a falcon can dive? _____

Name _____ **Date** _____

Activity 6

We need plants. Plants need people. People and plants are a winning team. People use **oxygen**. Oxygen is a gas in the air. People breathe in air. They use the oxygen in the air. They breathe out a different gas. They breathe out **carbon dioxide**.

Plants take in air too. Plants use the carbon dioxide in the air. What do plants let out? They let out oxygen!

From the story, you can tell that

   A. people do not need plants

   B. people use carbon dioxide in the air

   C. people and plants use the same gases in the air

   D. people and plants use different gases in the air

What might happen if all the forests were cut down?

   A. There would not be enough oxygen.

   B. There would not be enough carbon dioxide.

Write the words *oxygen* and *carbon dioxide* on the diagram. Make sure you write each word on the correct arrow.

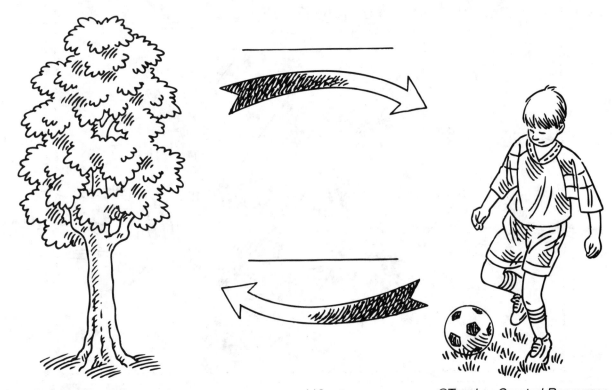

Name _____ **Date** _____

Activity 7

Rice is an important food. Half of the people in the world depend on rice. Rice first came from Southeast Asia. People have been growing rice for over 7,000 years.

People needed more land to grow enough rice. How did people make more land? They cut steps in mountains. The steps are large and flat. They are built up with stones. The stones stop the soil from eroding away.

Connect the dots. On what line is there more space to grow rice?

A.

B.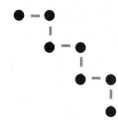

Color the countries that make up Southeast Asia: Myanmar, Thailand, Malaysia, Laos, Cambodia, Vietnam, Indonesia, Singapore, and the Philippines.

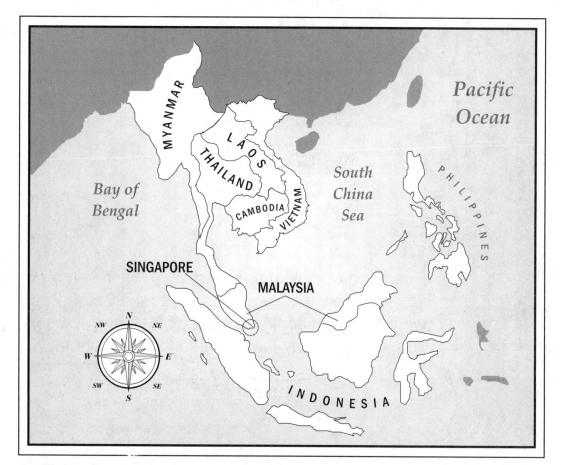

How Earth's Surface Shapes How People Live

What I Need to Know

Vocabulary

- adapt
- hazard
- hurricane
- earthquake

About Earth Shaping How People Live

Earth helps shape what we do. It may shape what we wear and how we dress. It may shape what we make or invent. It may shape how or where we build our houses.

There are natural hazards or dangers on Earth. We want to be safe. Often, we make or do things in special ways so that we are safe from natural hazards.

What I Do

Read and complete each Activity. When you are done, you will know who won the race to the South Pole, who were the first people to make clothes by cutting cloth, and you will know why they wanted to cut the cloth.

Name _____ **Date** _____

Activity 1

To make our clothes, we cut. We cut cloth.
We cut it to fit our forms. We cut it to fit our bodies. We
do not just wrap cloth around us.

Iran was once known as Persia. Long ago, the Persians
cut cloth. They cut it to fit forms. They cut it to fit their
bodies. They started our form of modern dress. Why
did the Persians do this? Why did they cut cloth and
fit it to forms? They wanted to feel comfortable. When did they want to feel
comfortable? When they were riding horses!

From the story, you can tell that

   A. a country name never
        changes

   B. people in Persia did not
        have horses

   C. people riding horses do not care
        what they wear

   D. long ago people cut cloth to fit their
        bodies

Find Iran on the map.

On which continent is Iran? _____

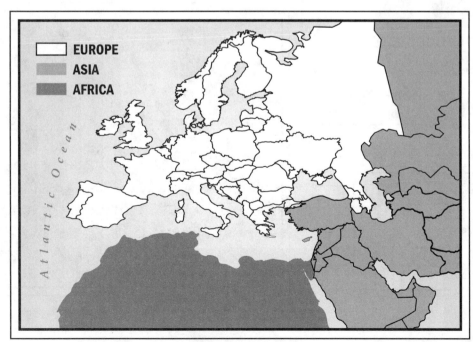

Name _____ **Date** _____

Activity 2

In hot climates, people can wear sandals. The sandals are open. The sandals help keep feet cool. In colder places, shoes cover feet. The covered shoes help keep feet warm.

Clogs are shoes. They have been around a long time. They have been around for over 2,000 years. Long ago, clogs were made of wood. A clog maker could make six pairs of clogs a day.

In the winter, hay was stuffed in the clogs. Why?

  A. There was not enough wood.

  B. The hay helped keep the feet warm.

  C. The hay had been around a long time.

  D. Clog makers needed to get rid of the hay.

Some clogs had holes in the sides. Why?

  A. Water could drain out.

  B. Shoes could be filled with water.

Many people in the Netherlands wore clogs. Find and color the Netherlands on the map.

Which continent is the Netherlands on? _____

What kind of shoes are you wearing? _____

Where were the shoes made?

_____

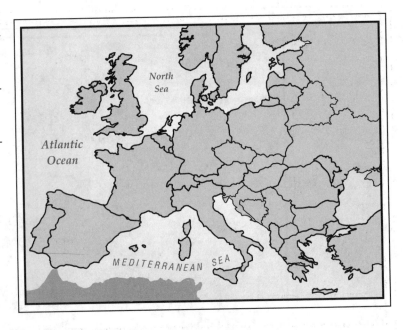

Name _____ **Date** _____

Activity 3

We are shaped by the world around us. We **adapt**. When we adapt, we change. We adapt to fit.   Think about what we wear. We adapt our clothes to fit where we live.

It was 1873. It was a cold day. Chester Greenwood was 15 years old. He wanted to ice skate. He couldn't ice skate. Why? His ears were too cold! They were so cold they hurt.

Chester went home. He made something. It protected his ears. It kept his ears warm. What did Chester make? He made earmuffs! He invented earmuffs. Chester's earmuffs are still being made today.

Chester lived in Maine. Maine was the 23rd state. Maine is the only state that borders only one other state.

Which state does Maine share a border with?

  A. Vermont   **B.** New York   **C.** Massachusetts   **D.** New Hampshire

Most likely, Chester invented earmuffs because he lived in a _____ place.

  A. hot   **B.** cold

How many states does your state share a border with? _____

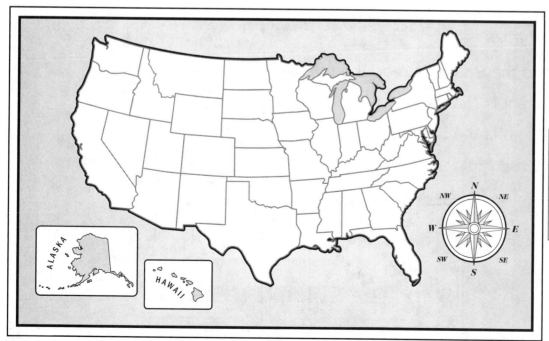

Name _____ **Date** _____

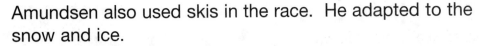

Activity 4

There was a race to the South Pole. An explorer named Roald Amundsen wanted to be first. So did a man named Robert Scott. Who would get there first?

Think about the South Pole. It is in Antarctica where it is cold and there is lots of ice. Who won the race? The man that adapted to the snow and ice won the race.

Amundsen used dogs in the race. The dogs pulled sleds. Amundsen learned from the Inuit how to use dogs. The Inuit live in the Arctic where they are used to living in snow and ice.

Amundsen also used skis in the race. He adapted to the snow and ice.

Scott brought tractors, but it was too cold for the tractors to run. Scott brought ponies, but it was too cold for the ponies as well. Scott did not use dogs to pull sleds. Instead he had his men pull them. Scott did not adapt to the snow and ice.

Who won the race?

A. Scott   **B.** Amundsen

Amundsen came from Norway. Skiing first became a sport in Norway.

Find Norway and the South Pole on the map.

On which continent is Norway? _____

On which continent is the South Pole?

_____

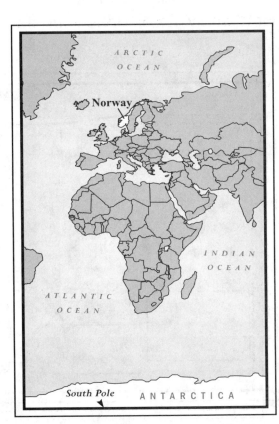

Name _____ **Date** _____

Activity 5

A **hazard** is a danger. Some hazards are natural. They are not man-made. They happen in nature. A natural hazard may be a **hurricane** or other big storm. Hurricanes start over the ocean.

We adapt our clothes to where we live. We also adapt to the hazards that might occur. For example, some houses in Belize are built on stilts. The houses are high off the ground. Why are the houses built on stilts? Hurricanes can strike Belize. A lot of rain falls. Water levels rise. High in the houses, people stay dry.

Answer *true* or *false*.

_____ A hurricane is a big storm.   _____ Hurricanes start over land

List some natural hazards where you live. _____

_____

What is one way you have adapted to the natural hazard? _____

_____

Find and color Belize on the map.

Which sea does Belize border? _____

On which continent is Belize? _____

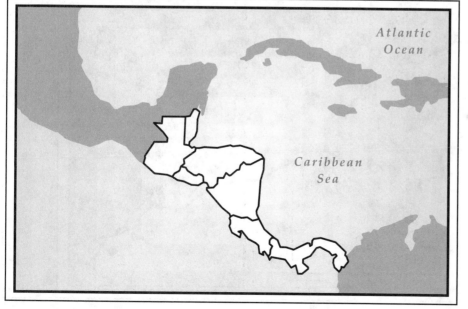

Name _____ **Date** _____

Activity 6

The largest oil field in North America is in Alaska. It is at Prudhoe Bay. A pipeline was built. It starts in Prudhoe Bay and all the way to Valdez. Oil flows through the pipeline. In Valdez, the oil is loaded into big oil tankers. The big ships take the oil away.

The pipeline crosses mountains, plains, and rivers. The pipeline is up on stilts. Why is it up on stilts? Moose and caribou live in Alaska. The moose and caribou migrate. They go south for the winter and go north for the summer. The moose and caribou go under the pipeline!

The pipeline was adapted to, or made to fit, Alaska

  A. by crossing rivers   **B.** by loading oil tankers

  C. by being built on stilts   **D.** by migrating moose and caribou

Find Prudhoe Bay. Draw a line from Prudhoe Bay to Valdez on the map.

Is Prudhoe Bay above or below the Arctic Circle? _____

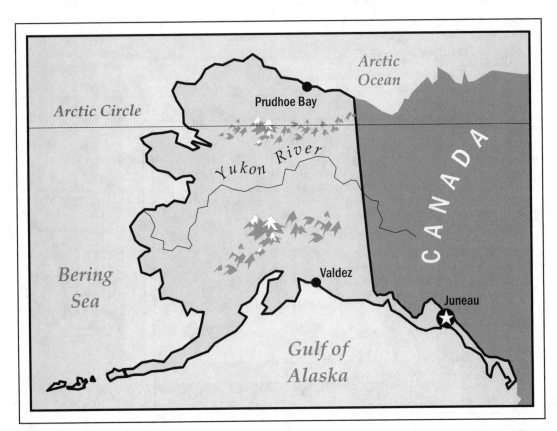

Name _____   **Date** _____

Activity 7

Earthquakes are natural hazards. An **earthquake** is when ground moves or shakes. Many earthquakes occur around the Pacific Ocean. Volcanoes erupt too. This area is called the Ring of Fire.

Which state is in the Ring of Fire?

A. Iowa   **B.** Delaware   **C.** Missouri   **D.** California

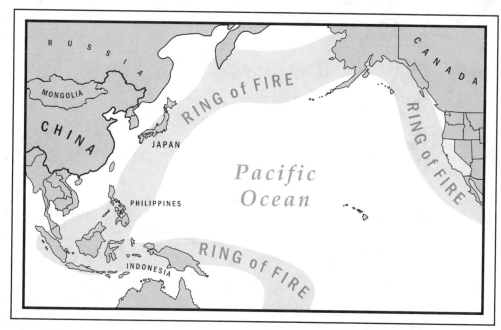

Some buildings are built to withstand earthquakes. Tall buildings are made to sway. The buildings sway back and forth. This stops them from falling down when the ground shakes.

The insides of buildings are adapted, too. For example, heavy objects are bolted, or stuck, to the wall. They are not put on shelves.

Why might a TV be bolted to a wall?

 A. so it can fall and hit someone if the building shakes

 B. so it can't fall and hit someone if the building shakes

Resources from Earth

About Earth's Resources

Earth has resources. It has supplies. It has things we use. All resources are not the same. A resource may be oil, trees, water, or land. Some places have many resources. Other places have fewer resources.

We use or want different resources at different times. Resources are moved. They are sold, bought, and traded. They are taken to where they will be used. Some resources are not renewable. Once they are used up, they are gone. To save our supply of resources, people recycle. They reuse the resources.

What I Need to Know

Vocabulary

- renewable
- nonrenewable
- recycle

What I Do

Read and complete each Activity. When you are done, you will know about a country where people were too good at catching fish, a waterfall with the highest water drop in the world, and where some diamonds are mined.

Name _____ **Date** _____

Activity 1

A resource is a supply of something. A natural resource is not man-made. It is found in nature. Fish are a natural resource.

Salmon are a kind of fish. These states are rich with salmon: Alaska, Washington State, California, and Oregon. Find the states on the map. Write an *S* on them.

Crabs are a kind of shellfish. These states are rich with crabs: Alaska, North Carolina, Maryland, and Louisiana. Find the states on the map. Write a *C* on them.

Lobsters arep a kind of shellfish. These states are rich with lobsters: Maine, Massachusetts, New York, and Florida. Find the states on the map. Write an *L* on them.

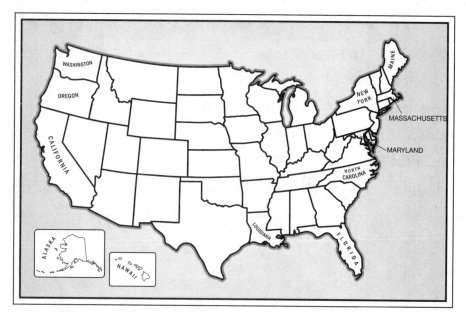

Draw a picture of a salmon, crab, or lobster in the box.

Are fish a natural resource in your state? _____

Do you think fish are natural resources in desert areas? _____

Name _____ **Date** _____

Activity 2

Iceland had a problem. What was the problem? They caught too many fish! How could this be?

Most people in Iceland have jobs with fish. They catch fish, or they work getting the fish ready to sell. The fish is sold to other countries. England buys a lot of the fish. Germany buys a lot of the fish.

Today, boats are better. Nets are bigger. It is easier to catch more fish.

People were catching too many fish. Soon there would not be any fish. There were no little fish to grow into big ones. There were no big fish to have little fish.

Iceland made new rules. The rules said that only so many fish could be caught. Iceland did one more thing. It did not let other countries fish near its shores.

From the story, you can tell that

A. people in Iceland want to stop fishing

B. Germany wants Iceland to catch more fish

C. England wants to fish in Iceland's waters

D. Iceland made rules to protect a natural resource

Find and label Iceland, England, and Germany on the map. (You may us **I**, **E**, and **G** to label.)

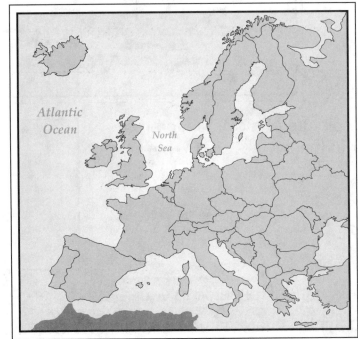

Name _____ **Date** _____

Activity 3

Long ago, there was only one kind of mammal on New Zealand. It could fly. It was the bat. Today, there are many mammals on New Zealand. There are people, dogs, cats, sheep, and cows.

Why do you think bats were the first mammals in New Zealand? (Find New Zealand on the map. Thinking about where New Zealand is will help you answer.)

  A. Bats could fly.

  B. Bats could hide on ships.

  C. Bats could ride on trucks.

  D. Bats could hang upside down from a railroad car.

The first people came to New Zealand in boats. People brought mammals when they came. New Zealand's land was a resource. Many sheep are raised on New Zealand. Many cows are raised, too. What does New Zealand sell to other countries? It sells dairy products!

List three dairy products.

  1. _____

  2. _____

  3. _____

Which continent is west of New Zealand? _____

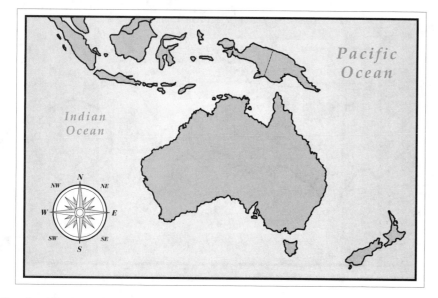

Name _____ **Date** _____

Activity 4

Some natural resources are **renewable**. We can get more, or we can grow more. Trees are a renewable resource.

Other resources are **nonrenewable**. We cannot get more. We cannot grow more. We can run out. Oil is a nonrenewable resource. We must use our nonrenewable resources carefully.

Underline the four renewable resources.

Circle the nonrenewable resources.

trees	wind	silver	oil	coal	land
gold	fish	copper	iron	diamonds	energy from the sun

Why must we use our nonrenewable resources carefully? _____

_____

Diamonds are mined in Arkansas. Find Arkansas on the map.

Which direction is Arkansas from where you are? _____

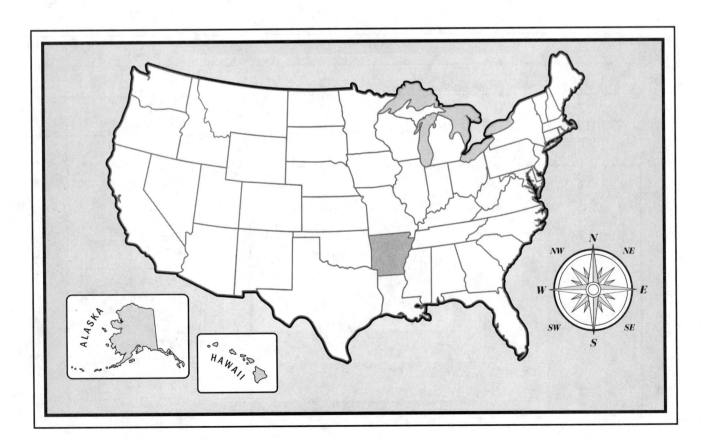

Name _____ **Date** _____

Activity 5

Some resources are not renewable. We cannot grow more or get more. Once it is used up, it is gone. Silver is not renewable. Gold is not renewable. Oil is not renewable.

How can we save our nonrenewable resources? We can use less. We can **recycle**. When we recycle, we use something again. We may use it in a different form.

Which is an example of recycling?

A. planting trees

B. building a house out of wood

C. walking more and using the car less

D. turning old plastic milk jugs into a bench

What does your city or school recycle? _____

_____

Name _____ **Date** _____

Activity 6

Finland makes paper. Paper is made from wood. Finland is one of the world's biggest paper makers.

What does this tell you about Finland's natural resources?

   A. Finland has a lot of oil.

   B. Finland has a lot of gold.

   C. Finland has a lot of fish.

   D. Finland has a lot of trees.

How much of Finland is covered in trees? Two-thirds. Color two parts of the block. That shows how much of Finland is covered in trees.

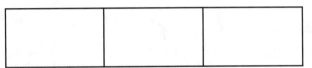

Finland is cutting down trees. It is making paper out of the trees. But Finland still has lots of trees. Why?

   A. Used paper is recycled.

   B. Many new trees are planted.

   C. Most of its paper is sold to other countries.

   D. Trees grow faster in Finland than in other places.

Find and label Finland on the map. On which continent is Finland?

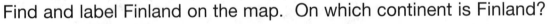

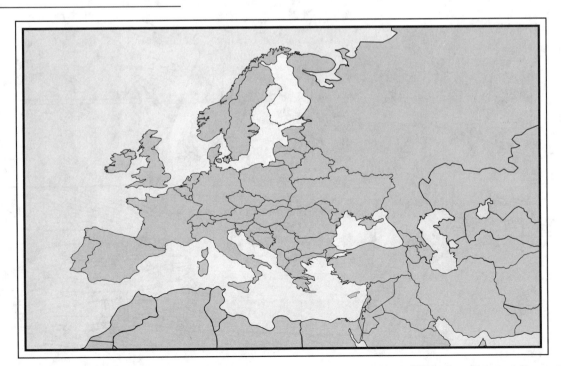

Name _____ **Date** _____

Activity 7

Many natural resources are moved. They are taken from one place to another. Countries trade. They trade, buy, and sell natural resources all the time. Venezuela has oil. The oil is shipped around the world.

Other natural resources cannot be moved. Instead, people go to them. Venezuela has Angel Falls. Angel Falls is a waterfall. It has the highest drop in the world. How far does the water drop? It drops 3,205 feet (977 m)! People come from far away to see this natural wonder.

What natural wonders do people come to see in your state? _____

_____

How does it help your state when people come to see natural wonders? _____

Find Venezuela on the map. On which continent is it? _____

Is it above or below the equator? _____

Which ocean does it border? _____

Understanding the Past

About Learning from Geography

Places change over time. They may change because people move in. The people may build houses or clear land. They may change when people leave.

We can use geography to learn about the past. We can study what the land was like. We can study how it changed. We can trace where people went long ago.

People may think one way about a place. Over time, the people may change. They may think differently. They may not feel the same about a place.

What I Need to Know

Vocabulary

- tourists
- immigrant

What I Do

Read and complete each Activity. When you are done, you will know about some homes that were built over 1,000 years ago, where the windiest place in the world is, and where four states meet in a corner.

Name _____ **Date** _____

Activity 1

Homes were built. 800 were built. The homes were built below cliffs. They were built along cliff walls. They were built side by side. They were built on top of each other. They were four stories high. They were like a big "apartment house." Who built these homes?

The Anasazi people did. This was long ago. This was over 1,000 years ago. The Anasazi lived in what is today New Mexico.

The "apartment house" in the story is near the city of Gallup. Find New Mexico. Find Gallup.

Santa Fe is the capital of New Mexico. Gallup is which direction from Santa Fe?

A. east   **B.** west   **C.** north   **D.** south

Jack has a job. What is Jack's job? He shows **tourists** where the Anasazi lived. Tourists are people who visit. They come to see new things. Jack tells

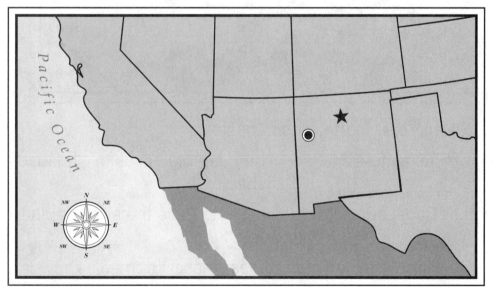

Jack's job most likely

   A. is over 1,000 years old

   B. started when tourists could come to visit

   C. was one of the first jobs in New Mexico

   D. would be the same in any place tourists visit

Name _____ **Date** _____

Activity 2

Mari's family took a trip. They took a trip to New Mexico. They did not go to work or live. They went to be tourists. Mari had a map. She marked where her family went on the map.

Look at the map. Follow the arrows to see where Mari's family went.

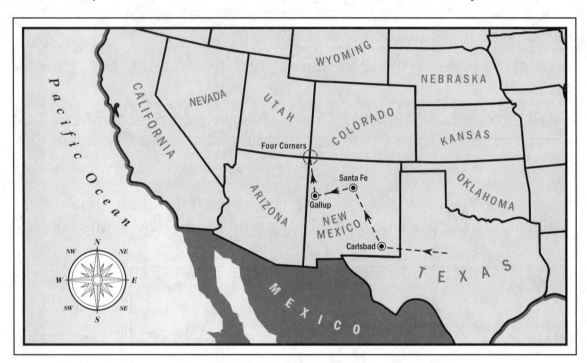

Fill in each blank with *east, west, north*, or *south*.

Mari's family drove from Texas to Carlsbad. There are big caves in Carlsbad. Mari's family drove to _____ Carlsbad.

Mari's family drove from Carlsbad to Santa Fe. Santa Fe is the state capital. Mari's family drove _____ to Santa Fe.

Mari's family drove to Gallup. They wanted to see Anasazi homes. They drove _____ to Gallup.

Mari's family drove to a point. It was a corner point. It is the only point where four state corners meet in the United States. They drove _____ to the Four Corners.

Which state corner does not meet at the Four Corners?

   A. Utah   **C.** Colorado

   B. Arizona   **D.** Oklahoma

Name _____ **Date** _____

Activity 3

Read the want ads below. The ads are for jobs.

Job 1

Wanted: Person to help sell clothes. The store is downtown. Please call 307-3201.

Job 2

Wanted: Person to work in new factory. The factory will be building furniture.
Please call 307-9800.

Job 3

Wanted: Person to help on fishing boat. The boat will leave from Trout Bay. Please call
329-5522.

Job 4

Wanted: Person to show tourists around. Tourists will be shown old fort buildings in Rock
Park. Please call 329-1324.

Look at the map. Where will the jobs most likely be found? Write 1, 2, 3, or 4
in each area.

For an area to have fishing jobs, the area

A. must be near trees   **C.** must be near parks

B. must be near farms   **D.** must be near water

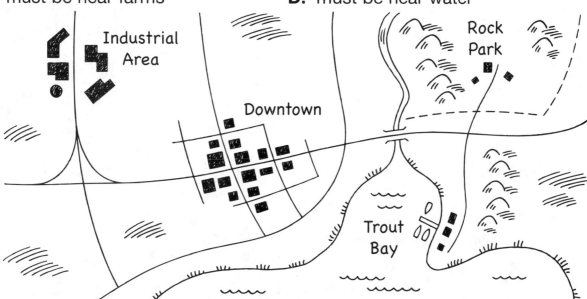

Name _____ **Date** _____

Activity 4

Dr. Rice is a meteorologist. A meteorologist studies the weather. Dr. Rice checks the weather at a weather station. The station is in New Hampshire. It is on Mt. Washington. The strongest wind in the world was recorded here. One gust reached 231 miles (372 km) per hour! Do you think Dr. Rice could live anywhere to do his job? Why or why not?

Think about the jobs in your state. List five jobs in your state.

1. _____

2. _____

3. _____

4. _____

5. _____

Circle the jobs you listed that were in your state long ago.

Today, are there more or fewer of these jobs in your state? _____

What is a job you would like to have when you are older? _____

Will you be able to live where you do now for your job? _____

Find Mt. Washington on the map.

Which direction is Mt. Washington from the capital of New Hampshire?

_____

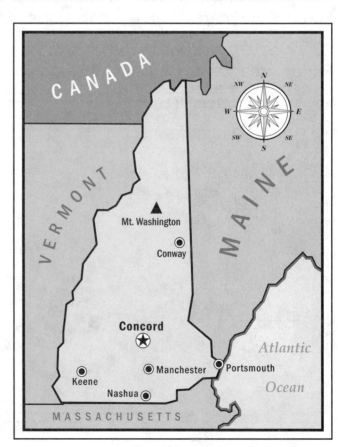

Name _____ **Date** _____

Activity 5

Ben Franklin was born in 1706. He was born in Boston, Massachusetts.
Find Boston on the map.

Ben moved to Philadelphia, Pennsylvania.

Draw an arrow from Boston to Philadelphia.

Ben then went to England.

Draw a line from Philadelphia to England.

Ben went back to Philadelphia.

Draw a line back to Philadelphia.

Ben went to France.

Draw a line to France.

Ben went back to Philadelphia.

Draw a line back to Philadelphia.

Ben was a printer, a writer, a statesman, and an inventor. Ben started the first public library.

Which ocean did Ben cross to get to England and France? _____

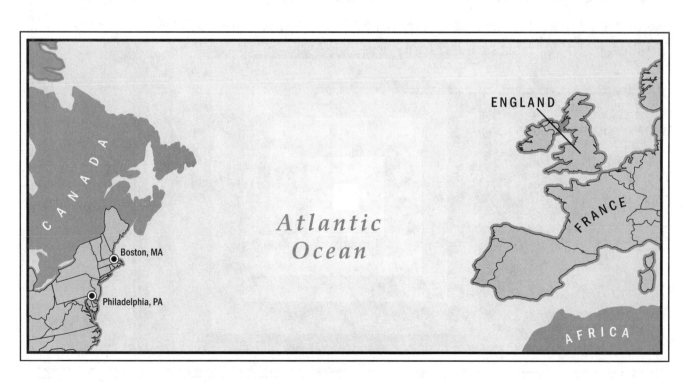

Name _____ **Date** _____

Activity 6

The way we think about places can change. At first a place is new. It is strange. We may not like it. Then we get used to it. It is no longer new. It is home.

The United States is home to many immigrant. An **immigrant** is a person who moves from one country to another. Kim moved. He lived in South Korea. He moved to the United States. In South Korea, Kim ate rice and kimchi for lunch. Many people eat kimchi in Korea. Kimchi is made of cabbage and other vegetables. It is made with ginger and other hot spices. Kim used chopsticks. He spoke Korean.

List two things that might be different for Kim in the United States.

   1. _____

   2. _____

Think of two ways you could make Kim feel at home.

   1. _____

   2. _____

Find Korea on the map. Find the United States.

Draw a line from Korea to the United States. Draw lines from other countries families from your class lived long ago.

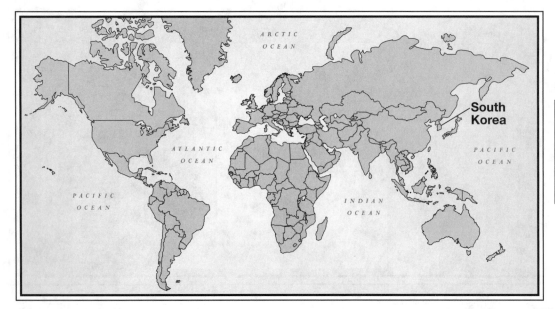

Name _____ **Date** _____

Activity 7

How old is a tree? You can tell its age by looking at its rings. Count the rings. The number of rings will tell you how old the tree is. Use each answer only once.

1. 5 years
2. 15 years
3. 10 years

_____ _____ _____

If a tree could talk, it could tell stories. It could tell us what life was like long ago.

Think about an old tree near you. In each box, draw what the tree might see. It might be a house, a person, or an animal. Or, write a story about what the tree might see.

Using Geography Today to Plan for the Future

What I Need to Know

Vocabulary

- population
- endangered
- extinct

About Planning for the Future

The future has not happened yet. It is going to happen. We can use geography to plan for it. How? We can look at populations. We can look at past numbers. We can look at present numbers. We can see if a population is likely to grow. We can think about what more or fewer people will need. We can think about how we should use our land and other natural resources.

What I Do

Read and complete each Activity. When you are done, you will know how the number of people in the world is changing, a mold that kills microbes and germs, and what people cut off of rhinoceroses.

Name _____ **Date** _____

Activity 1

The **population** is a number. It is a count of people. Different states have different populations.

On the map, find the states with the greatest human population. (These states had the most people living in them in 2004.)

Number the states. Color them blue.

1. California   **2.** Texas   **3.** New York   **4.** Florida   **5.** Illinois

On the map, find the states with the lowest populations. (These states had the fewest people living in them in 2004.)

Number the states. Color them red.

46. South Dakota   **47.** Alaska   **48.** North Dakota

49. Vermont   **50.** Wyoming

Why might more people live in California than Alaska? _____

_____

_____

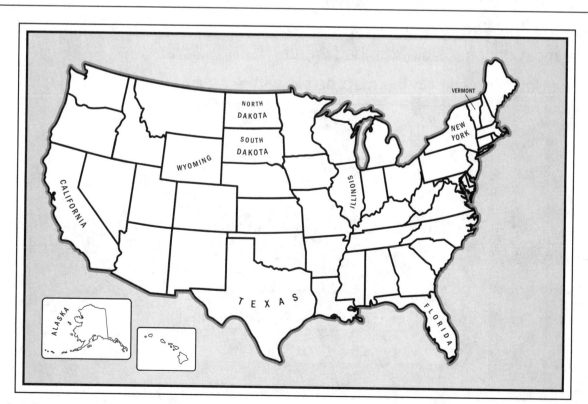

Name _____ **Date** _____

Activity 2

People need clean water. People live longer with clean water.

Long ago, many people got sick and were dying. It was 1854, in London, which is a city in England. In one area, over 500 people died in just 10 days.

John Snow was a doctor during that time. He thought about where the people were ill and how they were linked. All the people were getting water from the same well. The well water was bad!

Dr. Snow took the pump handle off the well. People had to go to a new place to get water. People stopped getting sick.

From the story, you can tell that in 1854

   A. many people had running water in their homes

   B. many people got their water from wells with hand pumps

From the story, you can learn that

   A. we must keep our water clean

   B. we must stop drinking well water

   C. we must not go to London

   D. we must only get sick from bad water

Mark London, England on the map below with a star.

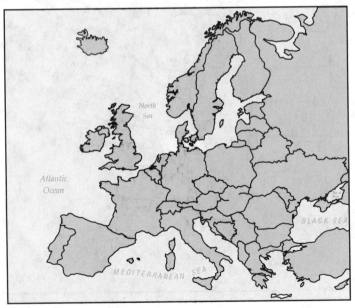

Name _____ **Date** _____

Activity 3

The population is growing. It is going up. The number of people in the world is growing. The graph shows the number of people in the world. It shows the world's population.

On the graph, color the dotted line. The line shows today's date. It shows the present. Write *present* at the top of the line.

Color to the left of the line. This shows the past. It shows what the population was before. Write *past* at the top of where you colored.

Color to the right of the line. This shows the future. The future will happen. The future is after today. Write *future* at the top of where you colored.

From the graph, you can tell that

   A. there are fewer people today than long ago

   B. there are more people today than long ago

   C. there will be fewer people in the world soon

   D. there are the same number of people today as long ago

If one is planning for the future, one should plan for

   A. fewer people   **B.** more people

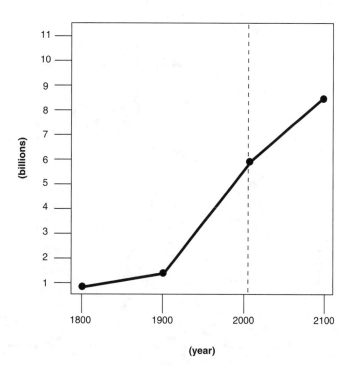

Name _____ **Date** _____

Activity 4

In 1922 a man blew his nose. The man was Alexander Fleming.
The man was curious. What would happen if he put his mucus
in a dish? Fleming was growing microbes, or little germs, in the
dish.

Fleming looked at the dish the next day. There were fewer
microbes! Something in Fleming's mucus was killing the
microbes. Fleming began to look for the germ-killing substance in other things.

After six years, Fleming found the substance. It was a kind of mold. Today we
call it penicillin. Many people are alive today because of penicillin. Penicillin
helps people fight germs.

The population is growing. Why is it growing? One reason is that we have
better healthcare. We have new medicines.

From the story, you can tell that

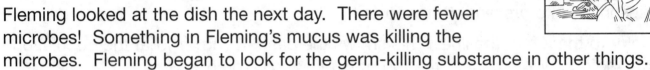

   A. Fleming blew his nose every day

   B. finding new medicines is fast and easy

   C. population can be linked to healthcare

   D. medicine is more important than clean water

Alexander Fleming was born in Scotland. Find Scotland on the map.

Which continent is Scotland part of? _____

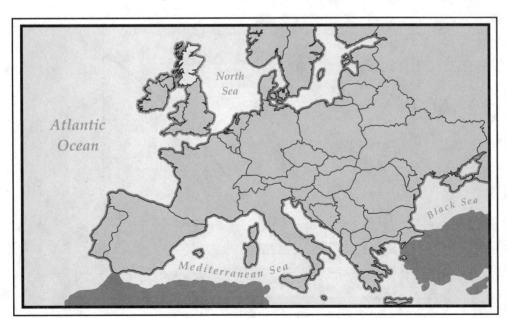

Name _____ **Date** _____

Activity 5

People need houses, schools, roads, and food. When people build or grow what they need, it takes up land. Animals can be pushed out of their homes. Animals may not be able to find things to eat.

Sometimes people kill animals for sport. Other times they kill them for their fur or other parts.

An animal can become **endangered**. Do you see the word *danger* in *endangered*?

Circle the word *danger* in *endangered*.

endangered

When an animal is endangered, it is in danger. It is danger of becoming **extinct**. When something is extinct, it is no longer alive. There are no more left.

The blue whale is big. It is the heaviest mammal in the world. One blue whale weighed 420,000 pounds (191 metric tons)! Almost all the blue whales were hunted. Laws were made that said the whales could not be hunted. The laws were made to save the whales from becoming extinct.

Blue whales feed in the Polar Regions (near the North and South Poles). They migrate closer to the equator to breed.

On the map, color where blue whales feed. Use arrows to show where they migrate to breed.

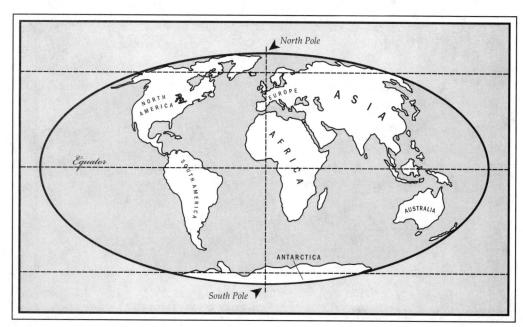

Name _____ **Date** _____

Activity 6

A rhinoceros is a big animal. There are five kinds. All the kinds are endangered. Rhinos are hunted. Why? People want their horns. They sell the horns. They get lots of money. People buy the horns. They think medicine can be made from the horns.

Rhinos use their horns to fight. They use them to plow the ground. They plow the ground when they are looking for mineral salts to eat.

How can people stop rhinos from being killed for their horns? People hunt the rhinos. They shoot them with a drug. The drug puts the rhinos to sleep. The horns are cut off. This does not hurt the rhino. It can grow a new horn. The rhino wakes up. It is free. It is safe from people who will kill it for its horn.

How can you stop an endangered animal from being hunted?

A. You can pay a lot of money for its fur.

B. You can not buy things made from it.

C. You can make sure there is not any clean water.

D. You can let people know you do not care about wild animals.

Rhinos live in Malaysia, India, and Africa. On the map, find and circle the places where rhinos live.

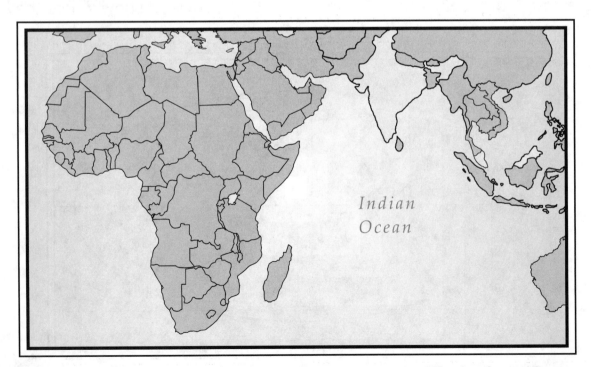

Name _____ **Date** _____

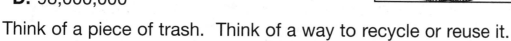

Activity 7

People in the United States make something. They make more than any other country. What do they make? They make trash. They make more trash than any other country.

With a growing population, why is it important to make less trash? (Pick two.)

A. Trash dumps smell nice.

B. Trash dumps take up space.

C. Endangered animals like to live in trash dumps.

D. Bad things from trash can leak into the ground.

To make less trash, people can use less. They can recycle too. One company has recycled plastic soda bottles. They have recycled over 98 million! What do they use the plastic for? They make fleece clothes!

Which number shows 98 million?

A. 980

B. 9,800

C. 98,000

D. 98,000,000

Think of a piece of trash. Think of a way to recycle or reuse it.

Draw a picture of the old trash and the recycled item.

Bibliography

Adams, Simon, et al. *The DK Geography of the World*. DK Publishing Inc., 1996.

"Anaconda," *Encyclopedia Britannica*, Encyclopedia Britannica Inc., 1990, 1:364.

Biel, Timothy Levi. *Zoobooks: Skunks and Their Relatives*. Wildlife Education Ltd., 1992.

————. *Zoobooks: Tigers*. Wildlife Education Ltd., 1992.

Brockenhauer, Mark, and Stephen Cunha. *Our Fifty States*. National Geographic Society, 2004.

Brust, Beth Wagner. *Zoobooks: Hippos*. Wildlife Education Ltd., 1989.

Cunkle, Lorna. *Extreme Nature Knowledge Cards*. Pomegranate Communications Inc., 2006.

Feresten, Nancy Laties, Director of Children's Publishing. *National Geographic United States Atlas for Young Explorers*. National Geographic Society, 1999.

Foster, Ruth. *Nonfiction Reading Comprehension Science: Grade 1*. Teacher Created Resources Inc., 2006.

————. *Nonfiction Reading Comprehension Science: Grade 2*. Teacher Created Resources Inc., 2006.

————. *Nonfiction Reading Comprehension Social Studies: Grade 4*. Teacher Created Resources Inc., 2006.

————. *Take Five Minutes: Fascinating Facts About Geography*. Teacher Created Materials Inc., 2003.

————. *Take Five Minutes: Fascinating Facts and Stories for Reading and Critical Thinking*. Teacher Created Materials Inc., 2001.

Gifford, Clive. *The Concise Geography Encyclopedia*. Kingfisher Publications, 2005.

Leo, Jacqueline, Editor-in-Chief. "Adventures in Turning Trash into Treasure," *Reader's Digest*, April 2006:24.

Mason, Antony. *People Around the World*. Houghton Mifflin Company, 2002.

McGeveran Jr., William, Editorial Director. *The World Almanac and Book of Facts 2006*. World Almanac Education Group Inc., 2005.

Siegel, Alice, and Margo McLoone. *The Birchbark Kid's Almanac of Geography*. Birchbark Press Inc., 2000.

Sipiera, Paul. *Globes*. Children's Press Inc., 1991.

Taylor, Murry. *Jumping Fire: A Smoke Jumper's Memoir of Fighting Fire*. Harcourt Inc., 2000.

Wexo, John Bonnet. *Zoobooks: Koalas*. Wildlife Education Ltd., 1988.

————. *Zoobooks: Lions*. Wildlife Education Ltd., 1989.

————. *Zoobooks: Seals and Sea Lions*. Wildlife Education Ltd., 1992.

————. *Zoobooks: Snakes*. Wildlife Education Ltd., 1992.

Wood, Linda, and Deane Rink. *Zoobooks: Bats*. Wildlife Education Ltd., 1989.

Zeman, Anne, and Kate Kelly. *Everything You Need to Know About Geography Homework*. Scholastic Inc., 1997.

Answer Key

Standard 1

Page 9: Activity 1: B
Page 10: Activity 2: A; D
Page 12: Activity 4: D; C
Page 13: Activity 5: D; C
Page 14: Activity 6: school: 2, store: 1, firestation: 6, park: 4, map would be too big to be useful
Page 15: Activity 7: south; east; north; east; north; west

Standard 2

Page 18: Activity 2: C; A; B
Page 19: Activity 3: C; south, west, north
Page 20: Activity 4: B; north; west; east
Page 21: Activity 5: 1; less
Page 22: Activity 6: North America; Africa

Standard 3

Page 25: Activity 1: B; D; north; west
Page 26: Activity 2: B; C
Page 27: Activity 3: D; B; A
Page 28: Activity 4: C; C
Page 29: Activity 5: B
Page 31: Activity 7: restroom and food area—wolverines, birds; seals—hippos, snakes, moose; koalas—wolverines, tigers; birds—snakes, restroom and food area, moose

Standard 4

Page 33: Activity 1: D; C
Page 34: Activity 2: C
Page 35: Activity 3: A; A; B
Page 36: Activity 4: B; cold, unable to grow things, hard to get around; B
Page 37: Activity 5: D; D
Page 38: Activity 6: B; B
Page 39: Activity 7: A and B; B; need water to drink and grow food; A

Standard 5

Page 41: Activity 1: C
Page 42: Activity 2: B; Asia—Japan, Pakistan; Europe—England, Denmark; North America—Mexico, United States
Page 43: Activity 3: Atlantic Ocean, Pacific Ocean, Arctic Ocean; Pacific Ocean, Arctic Ocean
Page 44: Activity 4: Arctic Ocean; Indian Ocean; Pacific Ocean; Atlantic Ocean
Page 45: Activity 5: South America; Pacific Ocean; Australia, Antarctica
Page 46: Activity 6: Caribbean Sea; Pacific Ocean; north; not connected to an ocean
Page 47: Activity 7: D; C

Standard 6

Page 51: Activity 3: C; B
Page 52: Activity 4: A; D
Page 54: Activity 6: B; D
Page 55: Activity 7: A; D

Standard 7

Page 57: Activity 1: B; A
Page 58: Activity 2: A; B; A; B
Page 59: Activity 3: North
Page 60: Activity 4: South; B
Page 62: Activity 6: Natural—ocean, rain forest, mountain, gulf; Man-Made—bridge, playground, road, canal; A
Page 63: Activity 7: B

Answer Key (cont.)

Standard 8

Page 65: Activity 1: C

Page 66: Activity 2: C; C; south

Page 67: Activity 3: Bats help plants and fruit grow. Monkeys eat the plants and fruit.

Page 68: Activity 4: C

Page 69: Activity 5: hawk, mouse, seeds; shark, seal, fish; wolf, rabbit, grass; wolf

Page 70: Activity 6: wolf (arrow) rabbit (arrow) grass; deer (arrow) grass; hawk (arrow) mouse (arrow) grass; mouse (arrow) insect (arrow) grass; hawk (arrow) bird (arrow) grass

Page 71: Activity 7: B; Africa, Mediterranean Sea; Atlantic Ocean

Standard 9

Page 74: Activity 2: C; A and C; Boston; East Coast

Page 76: Activity 4: 4; New York City and Mexico City; Sao Paulo and Buenos Aires

Page 77: Activity 5: B; B; there are roads

Page 78: Activity 6: Alaska; Gulf of Mexico; Rio Grande; Missouri River; Ohio-Allegheny River

Standard 10

Page 84: Activity 4: Asia; Europe; Africa

Page 85: Activity 5: C; C

Page 86: Activity 6: C; A; Asia; Indian Ocean; north

Page 87: Activity 7: D; Europe

Standard 11

Page 89: Activity 1: C

Page 90: Activity 2: C

Page 91: Activity 3: cars, tools, frames for buildings, bikes, etc.; because of weight, size, and location, most likely barge

Page 92: Activity 4: C; B

Page 94: Activity 6: oranges; cheese; cat food

Page 95: Activity 7: Africa; Atlantic Ocean

Standard 12

Page 97: Activity 1: C; D

Page 98: Activity 2: D

Page 99: Activity 3: A; Asia; north

Page 100: Activity 4: B; A; C; B

Page 101: Activity 5: B; B

Page 102: Activity 6: T; F; T; F; F; T; A

Page 103: Activity 7: A; C

Standard 13

Page 107: Activity 3: no; A

Page 108: Activity 4: Potomac River; A; D

Page 109: Activity 5: Thurston; King; C

Page 110: Activity 6: B; no light enters to warm or cool; always too dark to see

Page 111: Activity 7: more than

Standard 14

Page 113: Activity 1: B; D; north

Page 114: Activity 2: C; C; Asia

Page 115: Activity 3: Chart B; plants to eat, away from people

Page 116: Activity 4: C

Page 117: Activity 5: D; D

Page 118: Activity 6: D; A

Page 119: Activity 7: B

Answer Key (cont.)

Standard 15

Page 121: Activity 1: D; Asia
Page 122: Activity 2: B; A; Europe
Page 123: Activity 3: D; B
Page 124: Activity 4: B; Europe; Antarctica
Page 125: Activity 5: T; F; Caribbean Sea; North America
Page 126: Activity 6: C; above
Activity 127: D; B

Standard 16

Page 130 : Activity 2: D
Page 131: Activity 3: A; milk, ice cream, cheese, yogurt, butter, etc.; Australia
Page 132: Activity 4: renewable—trees, wind, fish, sun energy
Page 133: Activity 5: D
Page 134: Activity 6: D; B; Europe
Page 135: Activity 7: South America; above; Atlantic Ocean

Standard 17

Page 137: Activity 1: B; B
Page 138: Activity 2: west; north; west; north; D
Page 139: Activity 3: D
Page 140: Activity 4: north from Concord
Page 141: Activity 5: Atlantic Ocean
Page 143: Activity 7: 1, 3, 2

Standard 18

Page 146: Activity 2: B; A
Page 147: Activity 3: B; B
Page 148: Activity 4: C; Europe
Page 150: Activity 6: B
Page 151: Activity 7: B and D; D

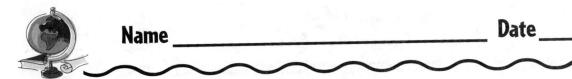

Vocabulary Practice

Standard 1: The World in Spatial Terms

Maps, Globes, and Finding Our Way Around

Fill in the missing word. Each word in the list is used once. If you need help, go back to the Activities for this unit. Look for the words in **bold** print.

compass	map	eclipse	scale	legend
globe	key	title	symbol	

1. Aristotle saw an _____ when the moon passed into the Earth's shadow.

2. A _____ is a round model of Earth.

3. A _____ is a flat picture of Earth or part of Earth.

4. The _____ of a map is a name that tells us what the map of.

5. A _____ shows us what symbols on a map stand for.

6. A _____ is the same as a key.

7. A _____ is used in a map key. We place it on a map to show where something is found.

8. A _____ shows directions. It shows north, south, east, and west.

9. On a map, the _____ shows us distance. It shows us what distance on the map is in the real world.

Vocabulary Practice *(cont.)*

Standards 2 and 3: The World in Spatial Terms

Mental Maps and Knowing Where We Are and Directions and Where Things Are

Diretions: Fill in the missing word. Each word in the list is used once. If you need help, go back to the Activities for these two units. Look for the words in bold print.

Australia	density	Asia	continent
South America	Africa	North America	Antarctica
mental map	Europe		

1. A map in your head is a _____ .

2. A _____ is a big land mass.

3 Hippos live on the continent of _____ .

4. Some seals live in the cold waters off _____ .

5. Wolverines live in _____ .

6. Tigers used to live all across _____ .

7. _____ is separated from Asia by the Ural Mountains.

8. Koala bears live in _____ .

9. Anaconda snakes live in _____ .

10. _____ is how many people or things live in one area.

Vocabulary *(cont.)*

Standard 4: Places and Regions

Different Places, Different People

Directions: Fill in the missing word. Each word in the list is used once. If you need help, go back to the Activities for this unit. Look for the words in **bold** print.

tropical grasslands	polar	erodes	valley
region	desert	cool grasslands	prairie
nomads	plain		

1. When something is being washed away by wind or water, it _____ .

2. A _____ is an area with little water.

3. People who do not stay in one place and move often are _____ .

4. A _____ is a large area of land.

5. _____ Regions are cold. They are lands of snow and ice.

6. A _____ is a treeless plain covered with grass.

7. A _____ is a nearly flat region of land.

8. _____ have warm summers and cold winters.

9. _____ are warm all year. They have wet and dry seasons.

10. A _____ is a low place. It is often between two hills.

Vocabulary Practice *(cont.)*

Standard 5: Places and Regions

Places with Things in Common

Directions: Fill in the missing word. Each word in the list is used once. If you need help, go back to the Activities for this unit. Look for the words in **bold** print.

> | | | | |
> |---|---|---|---|
> | ocean | canal | equator | rain forests |
> | goods | sea | coast | |

1. _____ are things you can make or sell.

2. A _____ is a ditch filled with water.

3. Land along a body of water is a _____.

4. A large, salty body of water is an _____.

5. A line that goes around Earth but is not real is the_____ . This line divides Earth into two parts.

6. Tropical _____ are hot, get lots of rain, and are near the equator.

7. A _____ is connected to an ocean, but it is smaller. It is salty.

Vocabulary Practice *(cont.)*

Standard 6: Places and Regions

How We Think About Different Places and Where We Live

Directions: Fill in the missing word. Each word in the list is used once. If you need help, go back to the Activities for this unit. Look for the words in bold print.

> bay   current   gulf

1. A _____ is a river of water that flows in the ocean. It can be cold. It can be warm.

2. A _____is a large area of sea that is partly surrounded by land.

3. A _____ is a small area of sea that is partly surrounded by land.

Standard 7: Physical Systems

Patterns on Earth's Surface

> axis   silt   Antarctic Circle   tilts
> Arctic Circle   canyon   swamp

1. The _____ is by the North Pole.

2. The _____ is by the South Pole.

3. Earth spins on its _____ .

4. When something _____, it leans.

5. A _____ is a wetland.

6. A _____ is a valley with steep sides. It has a flat bottom.

7. _____ is the dirt that running water dumps into standing water.

Name _____ **Date** _____

Vocabulary Practice *(cont.)*

Standards 8 and 9: Physical Systems and Human Systems

Where Animals and Plants Are Found and Where People Go

Directions: Fill in the missing word. Each word in the list is used once. If you need help, go back to the Activities for these two units. Look for the words in bold print.

> food web   suburb   ecosystem   food chain

1. An _____ is a system where plants and animals are linked.

2. A _____ shows what eats what.

3. A _____ shows how food chains are linked. It shows how animals and plants are linked in an ecosystem.

4. A _____ is a place just outside of the city where people live.

Standards 10 and 11: Human Systems

People Patterns and Buying and Selling Around the World

> capital   port   culture   barge

1. _____ is learned. It is how we dress. It is how we make our food. It is how we do things.

2. A _____ city is the city where the country or state government meets.

3. A _____ is a long, flat ship.

4. A _____ is a harbor. It is a place where ships load and unload.

Vocabulary Practice *(cont.)*

Standards 12 and 13: Human Systems

Where People Settle and How Earth Is Divided Up

Directions: Fill in the missing word. Each word in the list is used once. If you need help, go back to the Activities for this unit. Look for the words in bold print.

states	natural resource	counties
fertile	Washington, D.C.	country

1. Plants grow well in rich, _____ soil.

2. A _____ is not man-made. It is found in nature. It is a natural supply.

3. A _____ is a place with its own government. It is not a smaller part of another place.

4. The United States is made of 50 _____.

5. _____ is the capital city of the United States.

6. Often, states are divided into smaller parts. They are divided into _____ .

Standards 14 and 15: Environment and Society

How People Shape Earth's Surface and How Earth's Surface Shapes How People Live

carbon dioxide	earthquake	oxygen
hurricane	hazard	adapt

1. When we breathe in air, we use the _____ in it.

2. When plants take in air, they use the _____ in it.

3. When you _____ something, you change it to fit.

4. A _____ is a kind of danger.

5. A _____ is a big storm that starts over water.

6. An _____ is when the ground moves or shakes.

Vocabulary Practice *(cont.)*

Standards 16 and 17: **Environment and Society and The Uses of Geography**

Resources from Earth and Understanding the Past

Directions: Fill in the missing word. Each word in the list is used once. If you need help, go back to the Activities for this unit. Look for the words in bold print.

> tourist   recycle   nonrenewable   immigrant   renewable

1. When something is _____, we can grow or make more of it.

2. We cannot grow or make more _____ resources.

3. When we reuse an item or make it into something else, we _____ it.

4. A _____ is a person who visits a place to see new things.

5. An _____ is a person who moves to a new country to make a home.

Standard 18: **The Uses of Geography**

Using Geography Today to Plan for the Future

> extinct   endangered   population

1. The _____ is the number of how many people or things are in one place.

2. When something is _____, it is in danger of dying out.

3. When something is _____ , it is no longer alive. It is all gone.

Vocabulary Practice Answer Key

Standard 1—Page 156

1. eclipse 2. globe 3. map 4. title 5. key 6. legend 7. symbol 8. compass 9. scale

Standards 2 and 3—Page 157

1. mental map 2. continent 3. Africa 4. Antarctica 5. North America 6. Asia 7. Europe 8. Australia 9. South America 10. density

Standard 4—Page 158

1. erodes 2. desert 3. nomads 4. region 5. polar 6. prairie 7. plain 8. cool grasslands 9. tropical grasslands 10. valley

Standard 5—Page 159

1. goods 2. canal 3. coast 4. ocean 5. equator 6. rain forests 7. sea

Standard 6—Page 160

1. current 2. gulf 3. bay

Standard 7—Page 160

1. Arctic Circle 2. Antarctic Circle 3. axis 4. tilts 5. swamp 6. canyon 7. silt

Standards 8 and 9—Page 161

1. ecosystem 2. food chain 3. food web 4. suburb

Standards 10 and 11—Page 161

1. culture 2. capital 3. barge 4. port

Standards 12 and 13—Page 162

1. fertile 2. natural resource 3. country 4. states 5. Washington, D.C. 6. counties

Standards 14 and 15—Page 162

1. oxygen 2. carbon dioxide 3. adapt 4. hazard 5. hurricane 6. earthquake

Standards 16 and 17—Page 163

1. renewable 2. nonrenewable 3. recycle 4. tourist 5. immigrant

Standard 18—Page 164

1. population 2. endangered 3. extinct

Geography Word Log

Word	Meaning
------------------------------	--
------------------------------	--
------------------------------	--
------------------------------	--
------------------------------	--
------------------------------	--
------------------------------	--
------------------------------	--
------------------------------	--
------------------------------	--

World Map

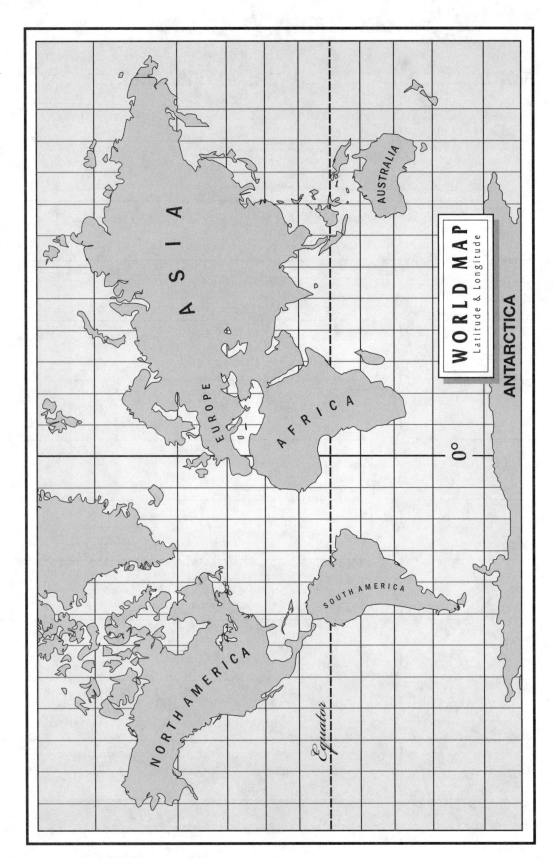

WORLD MAP
Latitude & Longitude

ASIA

AUSTRALIA

EUROPE

AFRICA

ANTARCTICA

0°

NORTH AMERICA

SOUTH AMERICA

Equator

Continent Map: Africa

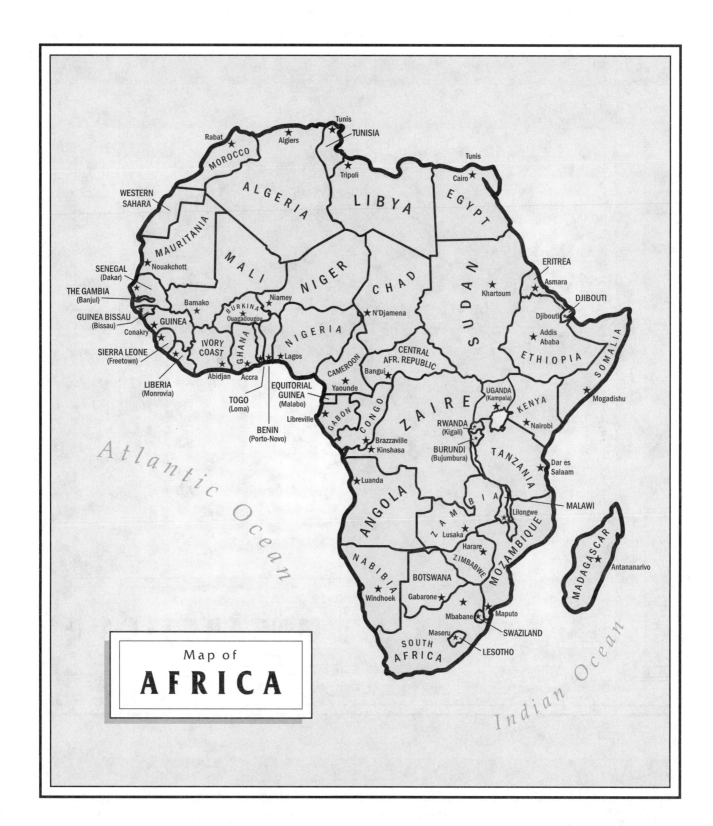

Tunis
TUNISIA
Rabat
Algiers
Tunis
MOROCCO
Tripoli
Cairo ★
WESTERN
SAHARA
ALGERIA
LIBYA
EGYPT
MAURITANIA
M A L I
NIGER
CHAD
S U D A N
ERITREA
Asmara
Nouakchott
SENEGAL
(Dakar)
Khartoum ★
DJIBOUTI
THE GAMBIA
(Banjul)
Bamako
Niamey
BURKINA
Ouagadougou
N'Djamena ★
Djibouti ★
GUINEA BISSAU
(Bissau)
GUINEA
Conakry
NIGERIA
Addis
Ababa ★
ETHIOPIA
SOMALIA
IVORY
COAST
GHANA
Lagos
CENTRAL
AFR. REPUBLIC
SIERRA LEONE
(Freetown)
Abidjan
Accra
CAMEROON
Bangui ★
UGANDA
(Kampala)
Mogadishu ★
LIBERIA
(Monrovia)
TOGO
(Loma)
EQUITORIAL
GUINEA
(Malabo)
Yaounde ★
ZAIRE
KENYA
Libreville ★
GABON
CONGO
RWANDA
(Kigali)
Nairobi ★
BENIN
(Porto-Novo)
Brazzaville ★
Kinshasa ★
BURUNDI
(Bujumbura)
TANZANIA
Dar es
Salaam ★
Luanda ★
MALAWI
Lilongwe
ANGOLA
Z A M B I A
MOZAMBIQUE
MADAGASCAR
Antananarivo
Lusaka ★
NABIBIA
BOTSWANA
Harare ★
ZIMBABWE
Windhoek ★
Gabarone ★
Mbabane ★
Maputo
SWAZILAND
Maseru ★
LESOTHO
SOUTH
AFRICA

Atlantic Ocean

Indian Ocean

Map of
AFRICA

Continent Map: Antarctica

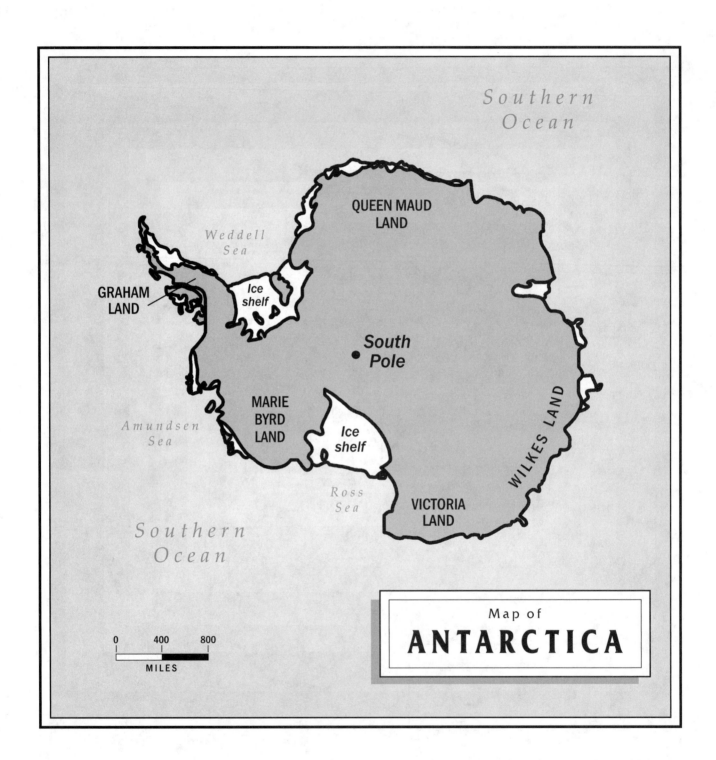

Southern
Ocean

QUEEN MAUD
LAND

*Weddell
Sea*

Ice
shelf

GRAHAM
LAND

South
Pole

MARIE
BYRD
LAND

*Amundsen
Sea*

Ice
shelf

WILKES LAND

*Ross
Sea*

VICTORIA
LAND

Southern
Ocean

0   400   800
MILES

Map of
ANTARCTICA

Continent Map: Asia

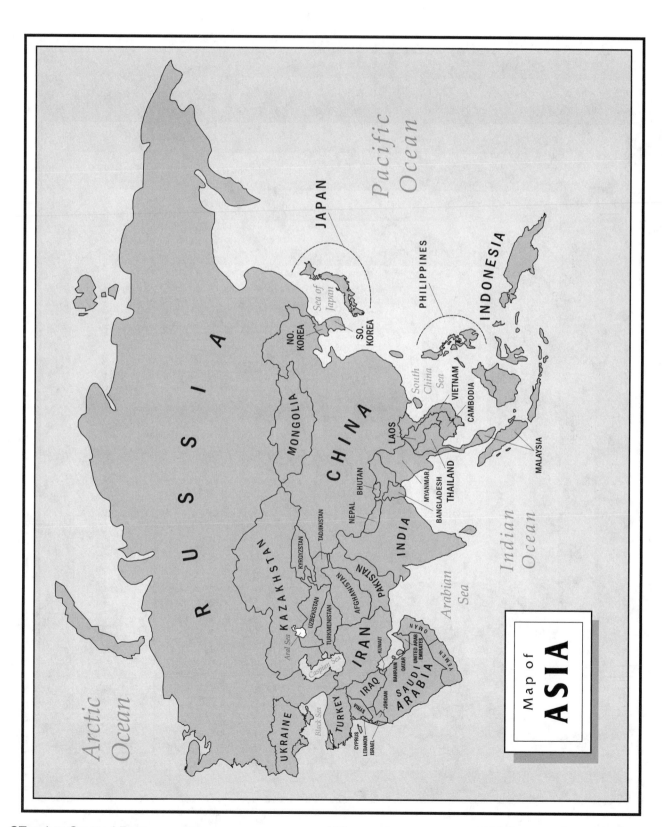

Map of
ASIA

Continent Map: Australia

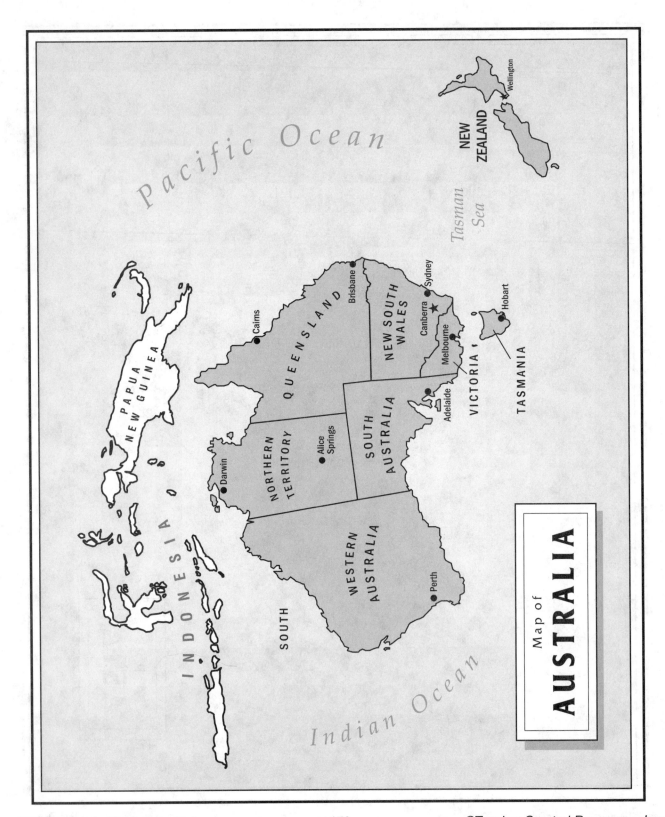

Pacific Ocean

NEW ZEALAND

Wellington

Tasman Sea

Brisbane

Sydney

Canberra ★

Hobart

QUEENSLAND

NEW SOUTH WALES

Melbourne

VICTORIA

TASMANIA

Cairns

PAPUA NEW GUINEA

NORTHERN TERRITORY

Alice Springs

SOUTH AUSTRALIA

Adelaide

Darwin

INDONESIA

WESTERN AUSTRALIA

Perth

SOUTH

Map of
AUSTRALIA

Indian Ocean

Continent Map: Europe

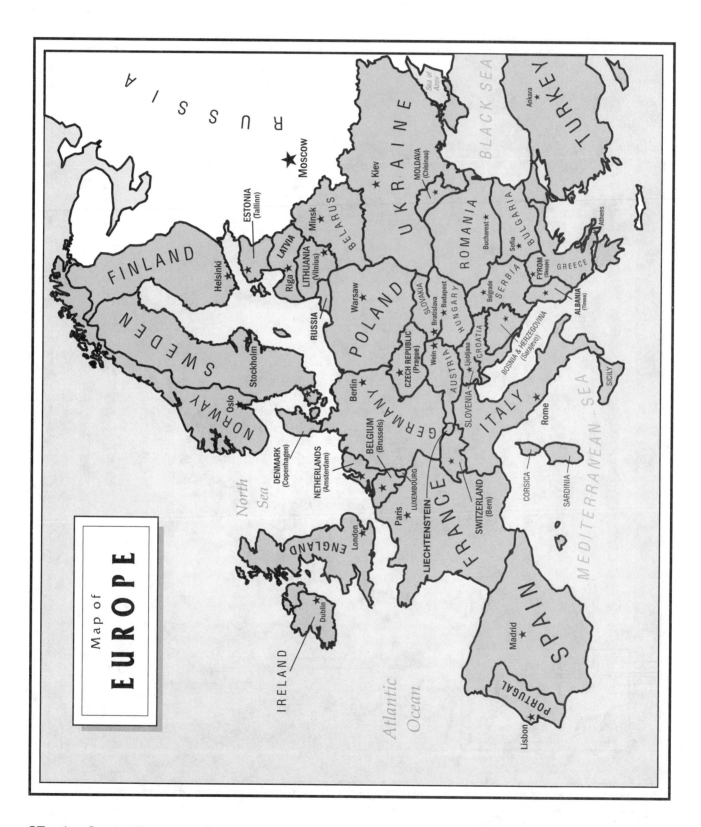

Map of
EUROPE

RUSSIA

Moscow ★

ESTONIA
(Tallinn)

FINLAND

Helsinki ★

SWEDEN

Stockholm ★

NORWAY

Oslo ★

LATVIA

Riga ★

LITHUANIA
(Vilnius)

Minsk ★

BELARUS

Kiev ★

UKRAINE

MOLDAVA
(Chisinau)

Sea of
Azov

BLACK SEA

TURKEY

Ankara ★

ROMANIA

Bucharest ★

BULGARIA

Sofia ★

SERBIA

Belgrade ★

FYROM
(Skopje)

GREECE

Athens ★

ALBANIA
(Tirana)

POLAND

Warsaw ★

SLOVAKIA

Budapest ★

HUNGARY

Bratislava ★

CZECH REPUBLIC
(Prague)

Wien ★

AUSTRIA

Ljubljana ★

CROATIA

SLOVENIA

BOSNIA & HERZEGOVINA
(Sarajevo)

DENMARK
(Copenhagen)

NETHERLANDS
(Amsterdam)

Berlin ★

GERMANY

BELGIUM
(Brussels)

North
Sea

ENGLAND

London ★

Paris ★

LUXEMBOURG

LIECHTENSTEIN

FRANCE

SWITZERLAND
(Bern)

ITALY

Rome ★

CORSICA

SARDINIA

MEDITERRANEAN SEA

SICILY

IRELAND

Dublin ★

Atlantic
Ocean

SPAIN

Madrid ★

PORTUGAL

Lisbon ★

Continent Map: North America

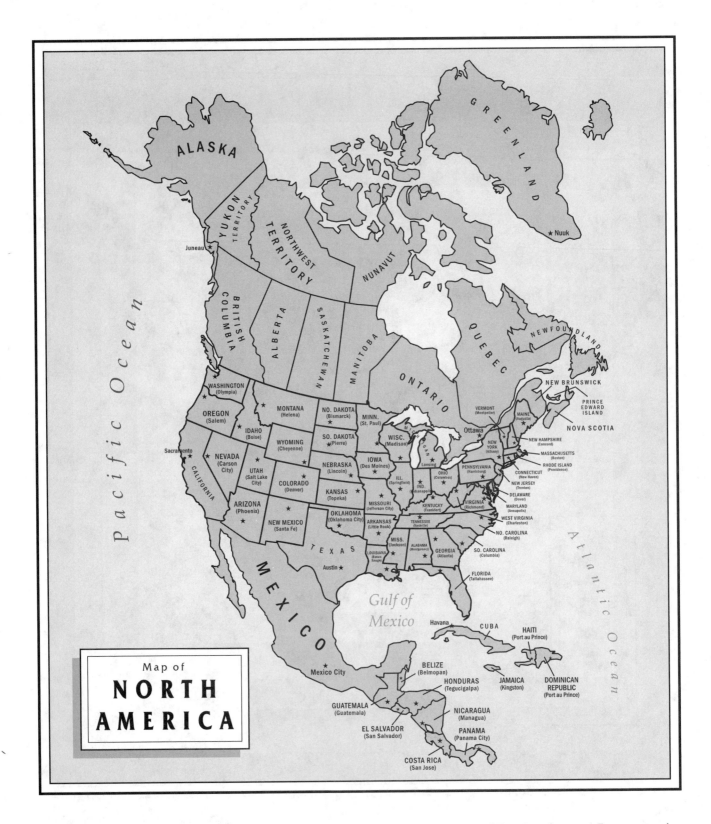

ALASKA

GREENLAND

YUKON TERRITORY

NORTHWEST TERRITORY

NUNAVUT

Juneau ★

Nuuk ★

Pacific Ocean

BRITISH COLUMBIA

ALBERTA

SASKATCHEWAN

MANITOBA

ONTARIO

QUEBEC

NEWFOUNDLAND

NEW BRUNSWICK

PRINCE EDWARD ISLAND

NOVA SCOTIA

WASHINGTON (Olympia)

OREGON (Salem)

MONTANA (Helena)

NO. DAKOTA (Bismarck)

MINN. (St. Paul)

VERMONT (Montpelier)

MAINE (Augusta)

IDAHO (Boise)

WYOMING (Cheyenne)

SO. DAKOTA (Pierre)

WISC. (Madison)

Ottawa

NEW HAMPSHIRE (Concord)

Sacramento ★

NEVADA (Carson City)

UTAH (Salt Lake City)

NEBRASKA (Lincoln)

IOWA (Des Moines)

Lansing

NEW YORK (Albany)

MASSACHUSETTS (Boston)

RHODE ISLAND (Providence)

CALIFORNIA

COLORADO (Denver)

KANSAS (Topeka)

ILL. (Springfield)

IND. (Indianapolis)

OHIO (Columbus)

PENNSYLVANIA (Harrisburg)

CONNECTICUT (New Haven)

NEW JERSEY (Trenton)

DELAWARE (Dover)

ARIZONA (Phoenix)

NEW MEXICO (Santa Fe)

OKLAHOMA (Oklahoma City)

MISSOURI (Jefferson City)

KENTUCKY (Frankfort)

VIRGINIA (Richmond)

MARYLAND (Annapolis)

WEST VIRGINIA (Charleston)

ARKANSAS (Little Rock)

TENNESSEE (Nashville)

NO. CAROLINA (Raleigh)

TEXAS

MISS. (Jackson)

ALABAMA (Montgomery)

GEORGIA (Atlanta)

SO. CAROLINA (Columbia)

Austin ★

LOUISIANA (Baton Rouge)

FLORIDA (Tallahassee)

MEXICO

Gulf of Mexico

Havana

CUBA

HAITI (Port au Prince)

Atlantic Ocean

Mexico City ★

BELIZE (Belmopan)

JAMAICA (Kingston)

DOMINICAN REPUBLIC (Port au Prince)

GUATEMALA (Guatemala)

HONDURAS (Tegucigalpa)

NICARAGUA (Managua)

EL SALVADOR (San Salvador)

PANAMA (Panama City)

COSTA RICA (San Jose)

Map of
NORTH AMERICA

Continent Map: South America

GUYANA
(Georgetown)

Caracas ★

SURINAME
(Paramaribo)

FRENCH
GUIANA
(Cayenne)

VENEZUELA

Bogota ★

COLOMBIA

ECUADOR

Quito ★

B R A Z I L

P E R U

Lima ★

La Paz ★

BOLIVIA

Brasilia ★

C H I L E

P A R A G U A Y

Asuncion ★

A R G E N T I N A

Pacific Ocean

Santiago ★

Buenos Aires ★

URUGUAY
(Montevideo)

Atlantic Ocean

FALKLAND
ISLANDS
(U.K.)

Stanley

Map of
**SOUTH
AMERICA**

U.S. Map

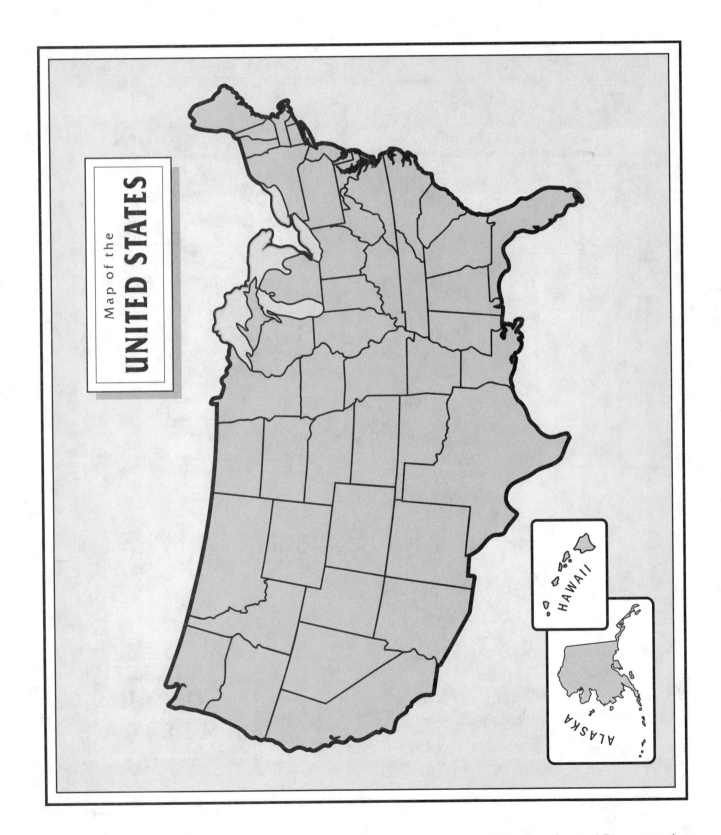

Map of the
UNITED STATES

HAWAII

ALASKA

U.S. Map

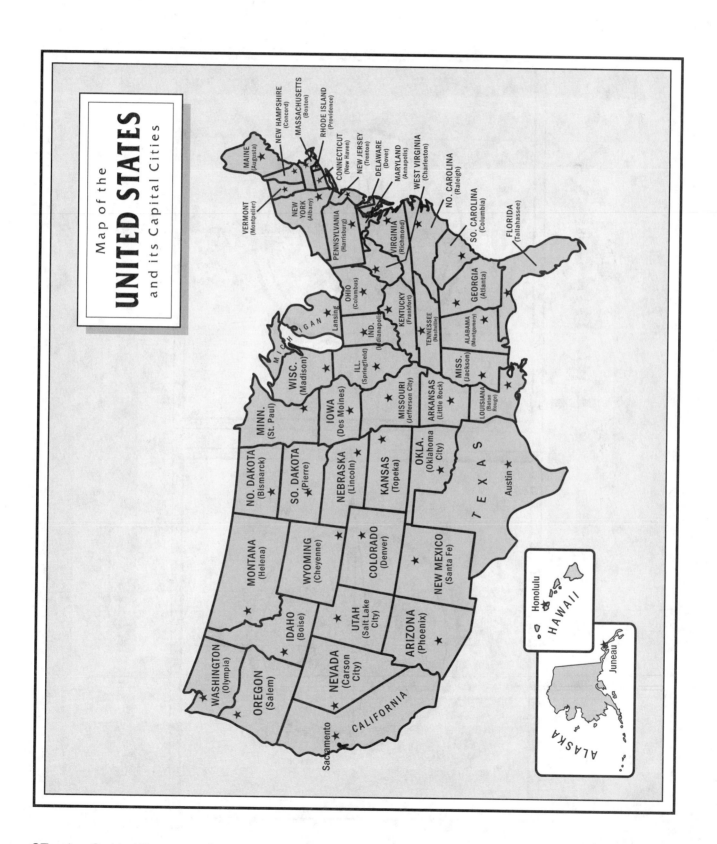

Compasses

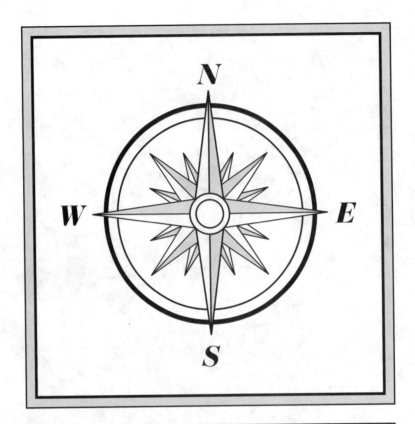

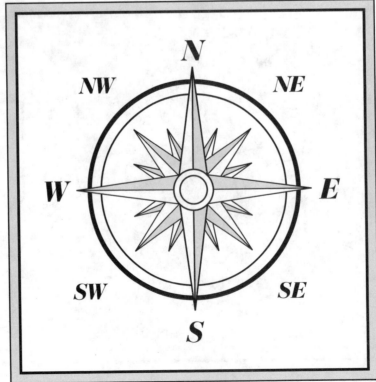